Journeys One
Religious Education
for Key Stage 3 Northern Ireland

Journeys One
Religious Education
for Key Stage 3 Northern Ireland

Francine Magill, Jill Hamill and Frances Boyd

The Publishers would like to thank the following for permission to reproduce copyright material:

Photo credits
p.2 (top left) © Pictorial Press Ltd/Alamy; (top centre) © Ruby/Alamy; (top right) © Rune Hellestad/Corbis; (bottom left) © Pictorial Press Ltd/Alamy; (bottom centre) © Allstar Picture Library/Alamy; (bottom right) © irish press photos/Alamy; **p.8** © Jim West/Alamy; **p.10** (far left) © Allstar Picture Library/Alamy; (left) © INTERFOTO Pressebildagentur/Alamy; (right) © Leo Mason/Alamy; (far right) © Stephen J. Boitano/Alamy; **p.12** (top) © Content Mine International/Alamy; (centre) © Content Mine International/Alamy; (bottom) © Pictorial Press Ltd/Alamy; **p.14** © Tim Graham/Alamy; **p.19** © Design Pics Inc./Alamy; **p.22** Logo courtesy of Malone College; **p.24** © Darren Matthews/Alamy; **p.25** © Francine Magill; **p.26** Logo courtesy of The Gideons; **p.29** Sistine Chapel Ceiling: Creation of Adam, 1510 (fresco) (post restoration), Buonarroti, Michelangelo (1475–1564)/Vatican Museums and Galleries, Vatican City, Italy/The Bridgeman Art Library; **p.38** © Niel Cooper/Alamy; **p.41** © The Print Collector/Alamy; **p.43** © Kerrick James/Alamy; **p.47** Ruth and Naomi, from a triptych, 2000 (oil on board), Wagner, Roger (b.1957) (Contemporary Artist)/Private Collection/The Bridgeman Art Library; **p.49** © TNT MAGAZINE/Alamy; **p.52** © Bettmann/Corbis; **p.53** © D. Hurst/Alamy; **p.55** Logos courtesy of Trocaire, CBM and Release International; **p.62** © Photos 12/Alamy; **p.63** Poster courtesy of Buy Nothing Christmas and Robert L. Peters; **p.64** © ImageClick, Inc./Alamy; **p.65** © 67photo/Alamy; **p.67** Courtesy of Ambassador Productions Ltd; **p.68** © Bettmann/Corbis; **p.70** Courtesy of Holy Cross Monastery; **p.73** © Jill Hamill; **p.74** (top) © Jill Hamill; (bottom) © Jill Hamill; **p.77** © John Mitchell/Alamy; **p.78** © Matthew Ashton/Alamy; **p.79** © Nathan Benn/Alamy; **p.80** (left) © Allstar Picture Library/Alamy; (centre) © Pictorial Press Ltd/Alamy; (right) © Pictorial Press Ltd/Alamy; **p.84** (top) © Francine Magill; (left) © Israel images/Alamy; (right) © INTERFOTO Pressebildagentur/Alamy; **p.85** (left) © Mary Evans Picture Library/Alamy; (right) © Nathan Benn/Alamy; **p.86** © Alan Gignoux/Alamy; **p.91** © Hemis/Alamy

Acknowledgements
Scripture quotations taken and adapted from the HOLY BIBLE, NEW INTERNATIONAL VERSION. Copyright © 1973, 1978, 1984 by International Bible Society. Used by permission of Hodder & Stoughton Publishers, a member of the Hachette Livre UK Group. All rights reserved. "NIV" is a registered trademark of International Bible Society. UK trademark number 1448790; **p.9** Lyrics of 'Who am I' by Mark Hall © 2003 Club Zoo Music/My Refuge Music/SWECS Music (EMI CMP)/For Europe: Small Stone Media BV, The Netherlands; **p.15** Extract from *Harry Potter and the Deathly Hallows* by J. K. Rowling (Bloomsbury, 2007) reproduced with permission from The Christopher Little Literary Agency and Bloomsbury, copyright © J. K. Rowling 2007; cover image from *Harry Potter and the Deathly Hallows* by J. K Rowling (Bloomsbury, 2007) reproduced with permission from The Christopher Little Literary Agency and Bloomsbury; **p.20** 'Man dies while saving dog!' taken from 'Bid to save dog likely took man's life' by Andrew Seymour and Chris Lackner. Reproduced with permission from *The Ottawa Citizen*; 'Man dies trying to save girlfriend's shoes' reproduced with permission of AFP and the Mail & Guardian Online (www.mg.co.za); **p.22** Quotes from pupils at Malone College reproduced with permission of Malone College; **p.62** *The Lion, the Witch and the Wardrobe* by C.S. Lewis copyright © C.S. Lewis Pte. Ltd. 1950. Extract reprinted with permission.

Every effort has been made to trace all copyright holders, but if any have been inadvertently overlooked the Publishers will be pleased to make the necessary arrangements at the first opportunity.

Although every effort has been made to ensure that website addresses are correct at time of going to press, Hodder Education cannot be held responsible for the content of any website mentioned in this book. It is sometimes possible to find a relocated web page by typing in the address of the home page for a website in the URL window of your browser.

Hachette Livre UK's policy is to use papers that are natural, renewable and recyclable products and made from wood grown in sustainable forests. The logging and manufacturing processes are expected to conform to the environmental regulations of the country of origin.

Orders: please contact Bookpoint Ltd, 130 Milton Park, Abingdon, Oxon OX14 4SB. Telephone: (44) 01235 827720. Fax: (44) 01235 400454. Lines are open 9.00–5.00, Monday to Saturday, with a 24-hour message answering service. Visit our website at www.hoddereducation.co.uk

© Francine Magill, Jill Hamill and Frances Boyd 2008
First published in 2008 by
Hodder Education,
Part of Hachette Livre UK
338 Euston Road
London NW1 3BH

Impression number   5 4 3 2 1

Year   2012 2011 2010 2009 2008

All rights reserved. Apart from any use permitted under UK copyright law, no part of this publication may be reproduced or transmitted in any form or by any means, electronic or mechanical, including photocopying and recording, or held within any information storage and retrieval system, without permission in writing from the publisher or under licence from the Copyright Licensing Agency Limited. Further details of such licences (for reprographic reproduction) may be obtained from the Copyright Licensing Agency Limited, Saffron House, 6–10 Kirby Street, London EC1N 8TS.

Cover photo Darwin Wiggett/All Canada Photos/Getty Images
Illustrations by Beehive Illustration and GreenGate Publishing Services
Typeset in Minion 13pt by GreenGate Publishing Services, Tonbridge, Kent
Printed in Italy

A catalogue record for this title is available from the British Library

ISBN: 978 0340 969 724

Contents

Welcome to readers — vii

Preface — viii

Introduction: What is Religious Education? — 2

Chapter 1 Who am I? — 5

    1.1 Introduction — 6
    1.2 Self-image 1 — 10
    1.3 Self-image 2 — 12
    1.4 No comparisons — 15
    The big task — 18

Chapter 2 The Bible — 19

    2.1 To die for! — 20
    2.2 What's so special about it? — 22
    2.3 Gideons International — 24
    2.4 No ordinary book! — 27
    2.5 A love story — 30
    The big task — 33

Chapter 3 Relationships – The story of Ruth — 35

    3.1 Overview — 36
    3.2 Faithfulness — 38
    3.3 Trust — 41
    3.4 Loving those who are different — 44
    The big task — 48

Chapter 4 Who is Jesus? — 49

4.1 Introduction — 50
4.2 Unique birth — 52
4.3 Unique mission — 54
4.4 Unique followers — 56
4.5 Unique power — 59
4.6 Unique death — 62
The big task — 64

Chapter 5 The Christian Church — 65

5.1 Pentecost — 66
5.2 The early Church — 69
5.3 Getting organised — 71
5.4 Full of diversity — 73
5.5 A dying community? — 75
The big task — 78

Chapter 6 Judaism — 79

6.1 Introduction — 80
6.2 Key beliefs — 82
6.3 The synagogue — 84
6.4 Important festivals (Passover) — 87
6.5 Bar Mitzvah — 90
The big task — 92

Glossary — 93

Index — 94

Welcome to readers

Welcome to your new school, welcome to Year 8 and welcome to a new RE textbook, written specially for pupils in Northern Ireland.

In school we want you to have learning experiences which will help you to develop, not just as a person, but as someone who will be able to make a useful contribution to society, the economy and the environment. We hope that the learning experiences you have in RE will help you to develop in these ways.

As you make your way through the book you'll discover that at the very beginning of each chapter the learning intentions are described. This means that you will discover right from the beginning what it is that you will be expected to know, understand and be able to do. This is just one part of a very important process called Assessment for Learning which your teachers will be using in school. There will also be opportunities for you to learn how to assess not just your own work but your friends' work as well.

Each chapter has a number of interesting and exciting activities for you to get involved in, sometimes on your own, but more often working in pairs, in groups or as a whole class. We hope that you will be willing to have a go at all these activities, that you will learn from each other and, most of all, that your learning will be fun.

Frances Boyd

Preface
Learning skills

In Chapters 1–6 you will find:

▶ **Learning intentions.** These tell you the skills and knowledge you will be learning in the chapter.

▶ **Skills and capabilities icons.** These show you at a glance where you have the opportunity to develop some cross-curricular skills. These icons are explained in the table below.

▶ **Get Active.** These are tasks which help you improve your thinking and practise your skills in Religious Education.

▶ **The big task.** This helps you pull together all your work at the end of the chapter and gives you the opportunity to reflect on your own performance.

▶ **Key words.** Bold terms are defined in a glossary at the back of the book.

Skill/Capability	Icon	Description
Managing information		Research and manage information effectively to investigate religious, moral and ethical issues, including using mathematics and using ICT where appropriate.
Thinking, problem solving, decision making		Show deeper understanding by thinking critically and flexibly, solving problems and making informed decisions.
Being creative		Demonstrate creativity and initiative when developing ideas and following them through.
Working with others		Work effectively with others.
Self-management		Demonstrate self-management by working systematically, persisting with tasks, evaluating and improving own performance.

Key elements

Throughout your Key Stage 3 Religious Education course you will also study ideas and concepts which help develop your understanding of the key elements of the curriculum, as shown in the table below.

Key element	Description
Personal understanding	Explore how religion has affected your personal identity, culture and lifestyle.
Mutual understanding	Investigate how religion has been selectively interpreted to create stereotypical perceptions and to justify views and actions.
Personal health	Investigate connections between religion and perceptions of personal health.
Moral character	Investigate individuals who are considered to have taken a significant moral stand and examine their motivation and legacy.
Spiritual awareness	Investigate and evaluate the spiritual beliefs and legacies of different religions.
Citizenship	Investigate how religion affects our contributions to society.
Cultural understanding	Investigate how religion affects our understanding of other cultures and other groups in our own culture.
Media awareness	Critically investigate and evaluate the impact of the media on religious belief.
Ethical awareness	Investigate ethical issues in religion or key figures who have behaved ethically or unethically.
Employability	Investigate how the skills developed through religious study will be useful in a range of careers, and consider careers associated with religious practice.
Economic awareness	Investigate the changing relation between religion and economic solvency.
Education for sustainable development	Investigate the active role that religion can play in the local and global environment.

Introduction: What is Religious Education?

> **Learning intentions**
>
> *In this chapter we will be learning:*
> - ▶ to appreciate that there are many different world religions
> - ▶ to understand the importance of studying Religious Education
> - ▶ to discover some basic information on each of the six major world faiths.

What do these people have in common?

Sarah Jessica Parker, Jewish *(American actress)*

Imran Khan, Muslim *(Pakistani cricketer and politician)*

Meera Syal, Hindu *(British writer and actress)*

Orlando Bloom, Buddhist *(British actor)*

Ben Kingsley, Quaker *(British actor)*

Mel Gibson, Catholic *(Australian actor)*

These people have a number of things in common. One is that each of them is associated with one of the world's main religious traditions.

Introduction

Get Active 1

1. Match each of the celebrities opposite with one of the world faiths below.

   Christian Sikh Jewish
   Hindu Muslim Buddhist

2. Match each of the symbols below with one of the world faiths above.

3. Write down one thing that you know about each world faith.

Religious Education is about asking questions, and this will mean that sometimes you leave a lesson with more questions than you began with.

It's about understanding where beliefs come from and why people view the world differently.

It's about weighing up different beliefs, opinions and experiences.

It's about you working out what you want to believe and why.

It's about exploring some of the oldest questions that have ever been asked, such as:

▶ Where did we come from?

▶ What is the meaning of life?

▶ Who or what created the world?

Information

Three-quarters of the world's population consider themselves to be religious.

That means that three in every four people across the world have a set of beliefs that they follow. Therefore it is important to explore and understand:

▶ What you believe and why.

▶ What others believe and why.

3

Introduction

Religious Education is not about telling you what to believe, but about helping you understand and explore your own faith and the faith of others.

Get Active 2

1. Write down three questions that you think should be asked in RE.

2. Look at the questions your partner has written, and choose two from the six that you would most like to know the answers to.

3. In groups of four, decide on one question that you would really like to discuss in class.

4. Write your question on a sticky note and collect them all on the board.

5. As a class, decide which question you want to discuss together.

Chapter 1
Who am I?

Discuss

▸ What is happening in this picture?
▸ What would you like to see when you look in the mirror?
▸ Are people always happy when they look at their reflection? Explain your answer.

Throughout your life the person that you are changes. Many things shape and influence you. You are not the same person you were when you were five, and you will not be the same person you are now when you are 25. The experiences you have, the people you meet, the things you learn, mould you into the person that you are right now. As you grow and have new experiences, meet new people and learn new things, you will change and develop. People's faith impacts on who they are, and therefore we will explore what Christians believe when they talk about being beautiful in the eyes of God and about all individuals being special and unique to God.

Chapter 1 Who am I?

> **Learning intentions**
>
> *In this chapter we will be learning:*
>
> ▶ to consider what the term 'identity' means
>
> ▶ to understand what self-image is and how sometimes others see us differently from how we see ourselves
>
> ▶ to explore what Christians believe it means to be beautiful in the eyes of God
>
> ▶ that Christians believe that all human beings are special and unique to God.

1.1 Introduction

In the midst of a great big world, full of different colours, shapes, sizes, objects and creatures, you and I exist. Human beings form a very important part of this planet – but why? What's so important about us? What makes us unique?

1.1 Introduction

Get Active 1

1. Spend five minutes considering and completing the following sentences:

   If I were a colour, I would be _____ because _____.
   If I were an animal, I would be a _____ because _____.
   If I were a sport, I would be _____ because _____.
   If I were a building, I would be _____ because _____.

2. Once you have completed the sentences, share your sentences with your partner. Does this exercise help to teach you anything new about your partner? If you, or your partner, come up with particularly good sentences, share them with the rest of the class. Sometimes it's difficult to describe ourselves, or identify what makes us different from others; this type of exercise often helps.

Sometimes when we are discussing who we are we talk about our '**identity**'. What do we mean by this term? One dictionary defines identity as: *The characteristics by which an individual is recognisable*. In other words, the things that make us who we are.

Get Active 2

One way of thinking about our identity is to consider the different roles we play in our lives. For example, you are a son or a daughter, you are a pupil, etc.

1. How many more roles do you play? In two minutes, note down as many of these as you can in a spider diagram.

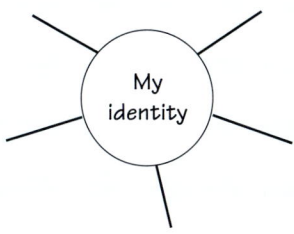

2. Now:
   Colour blue all the things you can control.
   Colour green all the things you can't control.
   Colour red the things you're not sure about.

3. How many did you get? Compare your findings with the people around you.

7

Chapter 1 Who am I?

What does the Bible say about who we are?

The Bible tells us many important things about who we are. Here are three particularly significant things it says about us:

▶ 1 Humans are part of God's creation. The Bible says that God chose to make us. We are not here by accident. The Bible also says that after God made human beings He said He was pleased with this part of His creation.

▶ 2 Human beings are made in the image of God. This is a difficult idea to understand. The simplest way to explain it is to use the example of families. Have you ever been told that you behave like your mum or dad? When people say that, they mean that you are particularly like one of your parents. When the Bible says that we are made in the image of God, it means that we are made to be like Him.

▶ 3 Humankind is loved by God. There are many, many passages that make this clear. For example, in the book of Romans it says that 'Nothing will be able to separate us from the love of God'.

Get Active 3

1 Look at the lyrics of the song 'Who am I?' by the Christian band, Casting Crowns on the next page.

In this song, the songwriter expresses his amazement that the God who created all things cares about him. The songwriter compares himself to who God is and is captivated by the idea that a being so far beyond him could have an interest in his life.

2 Think about some of the people who care about and are interested in you, even though sometimes you do not always treat them well. This is evidence of how valuable you are to them.

In your classwork books, complete the following sentences:

1 Identity means …

2 I am special because I am loved by …

3 Christians believe human beings are special because …

4 One Bible verse that makes it clear that God loves humans is …

Who am I

Who am I, that the Lord of all the earth
Would care to know my name
Would care to feel my hurt
Who am I, that the Bright and Morning Star
Would choose to light the way
For my ever wandering heart

Not because of who I am
But because of what You've done
Not because of what I've done
But because of who You are

Chorus:
I am a flower quickly fading
Here today and gone tomorrow
A wave tossed in the ocean
A vapour in the wind
Still You hear me when I'm calling
Lord, You catch me when I'm falling
And You've told me who I am
I am Yours, I am Yours

Who am I, that the eyes that see my sin
Would look on me with love and watch me rise again
Who am I, that the voice that calmed the sea
Would call out through the rain
And calm the storm in me

I am Yours
Whom shall I fear
Whom shall I fear
'Cause I am Yours
I am Yours

'Who am I' by Mark Hall © 2003 Club Zoo Music/My Refuge Music/SWECS Music (EMI CMP)/For Europe: Small Stone Media BV, The Netherlands

Chapter 1 Who am I?

1.2 Self-image 1

Have you ever been at a fairground where there is a 'House of Mirrors' – a room with different mirrors that change the way you look? The mirrors do not show us exactly how we look – they distort or change our appearance in different ways.

Sometimes when people think about themselves their image is distorted – in other words their image is not true to how others see them. This can happen in different ways – either they think overly positively about themselves, or else they see themselves very negatively.

Here are some quotations from the rich and famous who think very highly of themselves:

'I always thought I should be treated like a star.'
Madonna *(famous singer and dancer)*

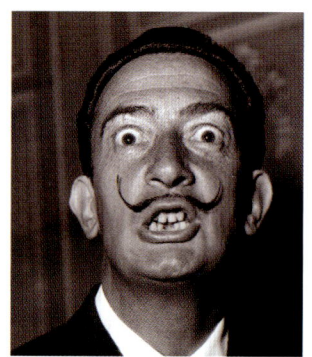

'Every morning when I wake up, I experience an exquisite joy – the joy of being Salvador Dalí – and I ask myself in rapture: What wonderful things this Salvador Dalí is going to accomplish today?'
Salvador Dalí *(famous Spanish painter)*

'I'm young, I'm fast, I'm pretty and I can't possibly be beat …'
Muhammad Ali *(American boxer – Olympic gold medallist and world heavyweight champion)*

'My greatest strength is that I have no weaknesses.'
John McEnroe *(American tennis player and sports commentator)*

Undoubtedly each person above was or is very successful. Yet we may find some of the attitudes they express unsatisfactory. Why is this?

Key word

Self-image – the way a person sees themselves, and the way they believe that others see them.

1.2 Self-image 1

Get Active 1

1. In life, we often encounter people who think very highly of themselves. Without identifying specific individuals, discuss in groups how people like this behave, what they say and what it is like to be around them.

2. Think of a situation that your group could role play in which one of the group displays the above characteristics. Try to show imaginatively how others around this person feel about their attitude.

The Bible makes it clear that no one should regard themselves as perfect or as better than others around them.

1 Corinthians 4: 7
For who makes you different from anyone else? What do you have that you did not receive? And if you did receive it, why do you boast as though you did not?

James 4: 16
All boasting is evil.

Proverbs 16: 18
Pride goes before destruction, a haughty spirit before a fall.

Get Active 2

Read the Bible quotes above then discuss, and write answers to, the questions below.

1. What does the Bible say about pride and boasting?

2. What do you think are some of the reasons that the Bible says that pride leads to destruction? What do you think this means?

3. When is it most difficult not to boast?

11

Chapter 1 Who am I?

1.3 Self-image 2

Watching TV is the UK's most popular leisure pastime. On average, people watch over 25 hours of television per week. Access to TV can be very important – television can be entertaining, informative and even educational.

However, TV viewing can also be very dangerous. It seems to tell us that we live in a world full of people with the perfect shape, clothes, image and talents. Many young people judge themselves against these standards – and this can lead to them having a very negative view of themselves.

These ideas are often played upon by advertising companies; very often they design their advertisements in such a way as to suggest to us that if we buy their product we will be more attractive, popular, beautiful, etc.

Most of us think that these women are very attractive. Why would they feel like this?

'I have a boy's body. I would prefer to have more curves because I think that's more beautiful. I would much rather have J. Lo's body than mine.'
Nicole Kidman

Get Active 1

Get into small groups of three to four pupils. You will be given a short period of time to create a mock TV commercial. Choose together the product you are going to advertise. Your completed commercial should last for no more than 30 seconds. Your goal is to try to sell your product to your audience by suggesting to them that this item – no matter how unrelated! – will improve their image.

'I loathe watching myself. You've got your own ugly mug staring back at you and it's a jarring sensation. I always think I'm like a man.'
Keira Knightley

The reality is that most people – even those we'd least expect – feel negatively about themselves in one way or another.

'I am odd-looking. I sometimes think I look like a funny Muppet.'
Angelina Jolie

1.3 Self-image 2

Read the following story:

The Lord said to Samuel, one of his followers, 'Go to Bethlehem, to a man named Jesse, because I have chosen one of his sons to be king.' Samuel did what the Lord said. When he arrived at Bethlehem he asked Jesse to gather his sons.

When they arrived, Samuel saw Jesse's son Eliab and thought, 'This man standing here in the Lord's presence is surely the one he has chosen.' But the Lord said to Samuel, 'Pay no attention to how tall and handsome he is. I have rejected him. I do not look at the things people look at. They look at the outward appearance, but I look at the heart.'

Then Jesse called his son Abinadab and brought him to Samuel. But Samuel said, 'The Lord hasn't chosen him either.' Jesse then brought Shammah, but Samuel said, 'No, the Lord hasn't chosen him either.' In this way Jesse brought seven of his sons to Samuel. And Samuel said to him, 'No, the Lord hasn't chosen any of these.' So Samuel asked Jesse, 'Have you any more sons?'

'There is still the youngest,' Jesse answered, 'but he is out taking care of the sheep.'

'Send for him,' Samuel said. So Jesse sent for him. He was a handsome, healthy young man, and his eyes sparkled. The Lord said to Samuel, 'This is the one!'

A SUMMARY OF 1 SAMUEL 16: 1–13

Get Active 2

Discuss:

1 What does this story suggest about the importance of appearance?

2 What is regarded here as being more important than looks?

3 What might this mean for people today?

Chapter 1 Who am I?

What does it really mean to be beautiful?

Mother Teresa was a nun who spent her life working with the poor, the sick and the homeless in the city of Calcutta (now Kolkata) in India. Her job was neither easy nor glamorous. It was often dirty, dangerous and disheartening. Yet, despite the many difficulties she faced, Mother Teresa never gave up on her work because she believed that each person she helped was, in her words, 'Jesus in disguise'.

In a fitting tribute to Mother Teresa after her death, Michael Coren of *The Financial Post* said, 'Though [she] was hardly physically attractive in the conventional sense, she was in fact the most beautiful woman in the world.'

Get Active 3

Discuss:

1. Why do you think Michael Coren described Mother Teresa as beautiful?

2. Find out some more information about Mother Teresa from the following websites:

   www.cnn.com/WORLD/9709/mother.teresa/index.html
   www.answers.com/topic/mother-teresa

3. Put together an A4 fact-file on Mother Teresa to portray her beauty. Give examples of the work that Mother Teresa did and why she did it. Include images of Mother Teresa and examples of some of the things she said.

14

1.4 No comparisons

One significant factor that leads young people to develop a poor self-image is that they compare themselves to others. If they think they are different from others in a particular way, they are likely to exaggerate this in their mind and feel negative about themselves because of it.

This point is illustrated in *Harry Potter and the Deathly Hallows*. Voldemort has divided his soul into seven pieces and hidden them in objects called Horcruxes. He can only be killed if each of the seven objects is destroyed. If the Horcrux is in danger of being destroyed Voldemort will try to protect them by projecting mental and physical images of things that the person who is trying to destroy it hates.

Ron and Harry have a locket which is a Horcrux and only Ron can destroy it. In order to protect this part of his soul Voldemort uses Ron's insecurities and compares Ron to Harry – something that Ron has tried not to think about.

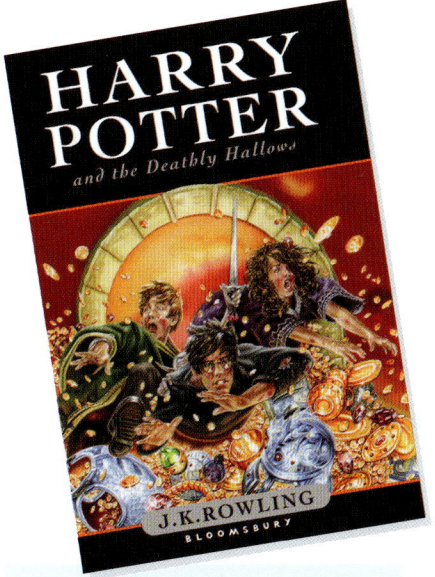

Who could look at you, who would ever look at you, beside Harry Potter? What have you ever done, compared with the Chosen One? What are you, compared with the Boy Who Lived?

J.K. Rowling, Harry Potter and the Deathly Hallows

Get Active 1

Think, pair, share

How do you think this makes Ron feel? Why does he feel like this? How could feeling like this affect his view of himself? How could feeling like this affect his relationship with Harry? Is there anything he could do to change how he feels?

Going deeper

Who do you compare yourself with …? Friends, family, the rich and famous?

What do you compare … your intelligence, looks, body shape, sporting ability, music ability, etc.?

How do you feel when you think you don't have what they have?

Chapter 1 Who am I?

The Bible says that God doesn't want people to compare themselves to others. What makes people valuable is the fact that they are so unique, as the following passage from the Bible illustrates.

PSALM 139: 1–6, 13–16

O LORD, you have searched me and you know me.

You know when I sit and when I rise; you perceive my thoughts from afar.

You discern my going out and my lying down; you are familiar with all my ways.

Before a word is on my tongue you know it completely, O LORD.

You hem me in—behind and before; you have laid your hand upon me.

Such knowledge is too wonderful for me, too lofty for me to attain.

For you created my inmost being; you knit me together in my mother's womb.

I praise you because I am fearfully and wonderfully made; your works are wonderful, I know that full well.

My frame was not hidden from you when I was made in the secret place.

When I was woven together in the depths of the earth, your eyes saw my unformed body.

All the days ordained for me were written in your book before one of them came to be.

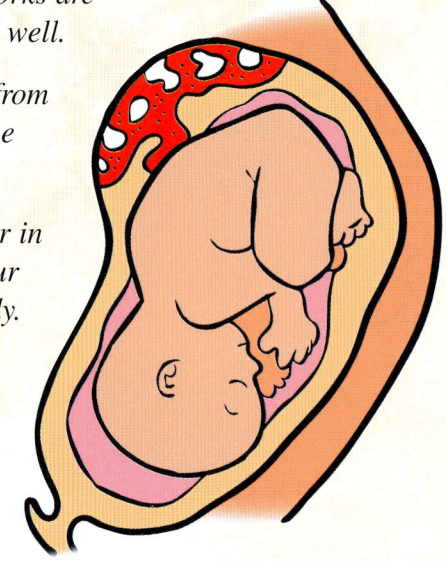

1.4 No comparisons

Get Active 2

1. Our fingerprints remind us that we are unique. There is no one else on earth that has a fingerprint that is identical to yours.

   Your teacher will provide you with paint or ink. Put some paint or ink on one of your fingers. Use this to create a fingerprint on a page in your classwork book.

2. Look at your fingerprint. See how it contains different circles. Draw a line from each circle and label it with a piece of information about you that makes you unique; for example, your eye colour, your favourite sports team, your nickname, etc.

3. Look at the drawings completed by other members of your class. See how each of you is different. These differences are not something to be ashamed of. They are something to celebrate.

Summary

Who am I?

The Bible says …

- ▶ You are made in the image of God and loved by Him.
- ▶ You are someone who is valued by God.
- ▶ You are beautiful in the eyes of God.
- ▶ You are unique and special to God.

17

Chapter 1 Who am I?

Who am I? The big task

Having completed the chapter on 'Who am I?', complete the following task:

Fill in a jigsaw map that represents who you are. Put your name in the middle of the puzzle. Using the information that you have discussed throughout the chapter, write a description of each of the following: my identity, the Bible and who I am, self-image, beautiful in God's eyes, self-worth, being unique.

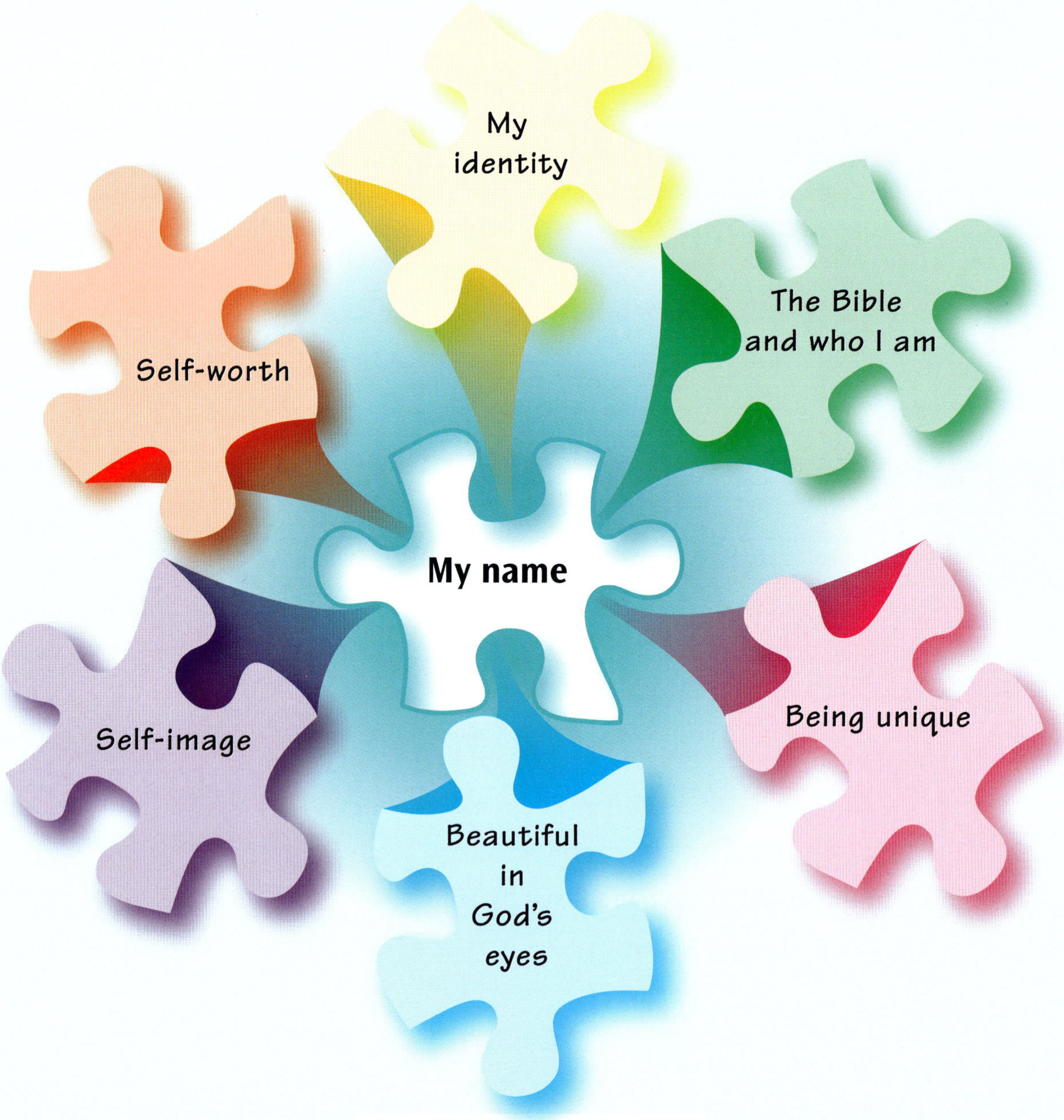

Chapter 2
The Bible

In *The Simpsons Movie*, Homer flicks through the Bible and then throws it away, saying that it has no answers in it. There are people today who hold this same opinion.

Yet others regard the Bible as the most important book ever to be written.

Discuss

▶ What are some of the reasons why people might value the Bible?
▶ Why do you think others might disagree?

There are no answers in here!

Chapter 2 The Bible

Learning intentions

In this chapter we will be learning:

▶ that the Bible is an important book to many people

▶ to understand that the Bible has changed many people's lives

▶ to identify that the Bible is made up of different types of books

▶ to recognise that Christians believe that the Bible is one way that God communicates with people

▶ to understand that the Gideons is one example of an organisation that tries to spread the Bible's influence throughout the world.

2.1 To die for!

Get Active 1

Is there anything that you would be prepared to die for?
Read the newspaper articles below and decide whether or not you would react in the same way.

An Ottawa man is missing and presumed drowned after floating away in the fast-moving current of the Ottawa River while trying to rescue his dog yesterday.

Peter Borodchak, 47, was last seen clinging to an ice floe and barely able to keep his head above water as he was swept away yesterday morning.

(From 'Bid to save dog likely took man's life' by Andrew Seymour and Chris Lackner, *The Ottawa Citizen*, 29 March 2006)

Man dies trying to save girlfriend's shoes

A drunk man drowned on Monday after jumping off the dockside into the river Ouse in northern England to rescue his girlfriend's shoes, the coastguard said.

The 21-year-old, whose identity has not been released, dived into the water at Goole, East Yorkshire, at about 1am after he and his girlfriend had spent a night out drinking heavily.

The woman alerted police when he failed to re-emerge. Police launched a sea and air search, including using an infrared camera.

A team of police divers eventually recovered the man's body at 4.40am.

(From AFP and the Mail & Guardian Online (www.mg.co.za), 18 April 2006)

20

2.1 To die for!

Throughout history, there have been many hundreds of men and women who have been prepared to make sacrifices, or even die, for the sake of spreading Bibles all over the world. Dumitru Duduman is one of these people. Read his story:

Dumitru Duduman was a Christian from Romania who spent many years trying to smuggle Bibles into Russia. He was imprisoned and tortured on many occasions because of his work – but he would not give up on his mission. Dumitru continued his work despite being seriously injured during his time in prison. Dumitru tells of many times when God protected him. For example, Dumitru believed that on one occasion God blinded the eyes of the police so they would not see the car filled with Bibles that he was riding in. Over a fifteen-year period, Dumitru smuggled more than 300,000 Bibles and New Testaments into Russia alone, not taking into account the number of Bibles that he distributed throughout Romania. He was eventually forced to leave his home country because his government did not approve of the work that he was doing. He ended up living in California, and there he preached and tried to spread the word of God until the day that he died.

Would you be prepared to die for a book?

Get Active 2

The story above is just one of many stories of Christians being persecuted on account of the Bible.

Complete one of the following tasks:

1. Write an email to Dumitru encouraging him to continue in his efforts to distribute Bibles in places where the Bible is banned.
2. Write an email to Dumitru in which you ask him why he thinks this job is important and worth risking his life for.

Success criteria

Discuss with your teacher what would make your email a good piece of work. Decide on a list of 'success criteria' and ensure you fulfil these as you complete your task. Here's an example of what a success criterion could be:

Your email should be formatted appropriately, with your email address, Dumitru's email address and a subject line.

21

Chapter 2 The Bible

2.2 What's so special about it?

Often, when people consider the Bible, they think of it as an ancient book of stories that are not relevant to modern society. Many people regard it as outdated and difficult to understand. Yet, in contrast to this, there are many others who regard the Bible as vitally important for their lives.

These people come from a whole variety of walks of life but each believes that the Bible contains relevant messages for them. Here are a few examples:

I think the Bible is special because it's God's word and it's one way He communicates with us. It tells us the way He wants us to live. It tells us that He loves us.
Jonathan, pupil of Malone College

I don't think the Bible is special or significant at all. It is just a book compiled of people's views of Jesus. I think it is untrustworthy and it is probably completely different to what the people actually saw – if they were real!
Matthew, pupil of Malone College

I don't think the Bible is special because it's just another book written by lots of people. Those people might not have written the truth and just written their own opinion.
Kirsty, pupil of Malone College

I think that the Bible is special because it tells us that God is special. It teaches us how God loves us and that we are special as well. The Bible is the most important book I have heard of.
Lauren, pupil of Malone College

Get Active 1

Discuss:

1 Which of the comments above do you find most interesting?

2 Do you agree with any of these quotations?

3 Are there ones you disagree with? Why?

4 Write your own statement about the Bible outlining what you believe and why.

22

2.2 What's so special about it?

Christians believe that the Bible is an extremely important book. They consider it to be one of the main ways that God speaks to them. They read the Bible when they need encouragement, comfort, guidance and answers. Christians believe that it gives advice about every situation in life.

> **Psalm 119: 105**
> *Your word is a lamp to my feet and a light for my path.*

Christians have to **interpret** what the Bible's teachings mean for their lives today. Different Christians have sometimes got different views on how certain passages should be understood. Can you think of an issue that Christians disagree on?

Do you know what the word 'interpret' means? If not, ask your teacher to explain it for you.

Get Active 2

Read the following letter that has been written to an Agony Aunt in a Christian magazine. Write a reply to the letter that offers advice on how Christians should respond to the problem. Look up the Bible references below to help you consider what guidance God gives.

Bible references: Ephesians 4: 31–32, Proverbs 12: 17, 19, 22

> Dear Sue,
>
> I have crashed the bike that my brother and I share. The front wheel has completely buckled. My parents are going to be really angry. I'm always so careful with the bike that they'll never suspect it was me, so I thought I would just let my brother take the blame. He'll deny it was him of course, but no one will believe him. He's always getting into trouble, and getting me into trouble too. It's payback time. I'm not being unfair, am I?
>
> Pete

23

Chapter 2 The Bible

2.3 Gideons International

One day during the year the Gideons will come to your school. They believe that the Bible is so special that they distribute a copy of the Bible to all Year 8s throughout Northern Ireland.

Get Active 1

If you had a very important message, how would you pass it on to others? Think of five different ways you could do this. Give the advantages and disadvantages of each. For example, if you created a website and posted the message on that, the whole world could look at it. However, how would you encourage people to log on to the site? How would you let people know that the site existed?

Why is this relevant?

The Gideons believe that one of the best ways to spread the message of God is by giving Bibles to people and providing Bibles for people's use in many places such as hotels, hospitals and prisons. If people own their own Bible, or have access to one, they can look at it whenever they feel they need comfort or advice.

The Gideons Bible. What do you think the Gideons logo stands for?

24

2.3 Gideons International

Sam and Jean are Gideons, and they are going to give us some information about the movement.

Why did you decide to become a Gideon?
Jean and I were living in Ballymena when a friend invited us to a new members' dinner. We listened to different people speak about the work that the Gideons do and we decided that we would like to get involved. That was in 1975.

Sam and Jean McEwen

How do you become a Gideon?
Once you have been invited to a new members' dinner and have decided that you would like to join, an application form is completed. Your minister will also write a letter of recommendation outlining your Christian commitment. This will be sent to Headquarters in England where the application form is processed.

Can anyone become a Gideon?
It is an organisation for business and professional men. Membership is also open to the wives of Gideons.

What does the work of the Gideons involve?
We give out Bibles to many people, not just school pupils. We also place them in lots of different waiting areas, such as dentists' and solicitors' offices. They are also placed in many buildings such as hospitals, prisons, hotels, oil rigs and libraries.

Where does the money come from to pay for the Bibles?
As a Gideon you pay an annual fee, and at our monthly meetings an offering is given. Anyone who is interested in the work of the Gideons can also give a gift.

The last and most important question: What is the aim of the Gideons?
To help people discover God and develop a living relationship with Him through reading the Bible.

Chapter 2 The Bible

Get Active 2

Look at the following mind map. With a partner, use it to explain two areas to each other about what and who the Gideons are.

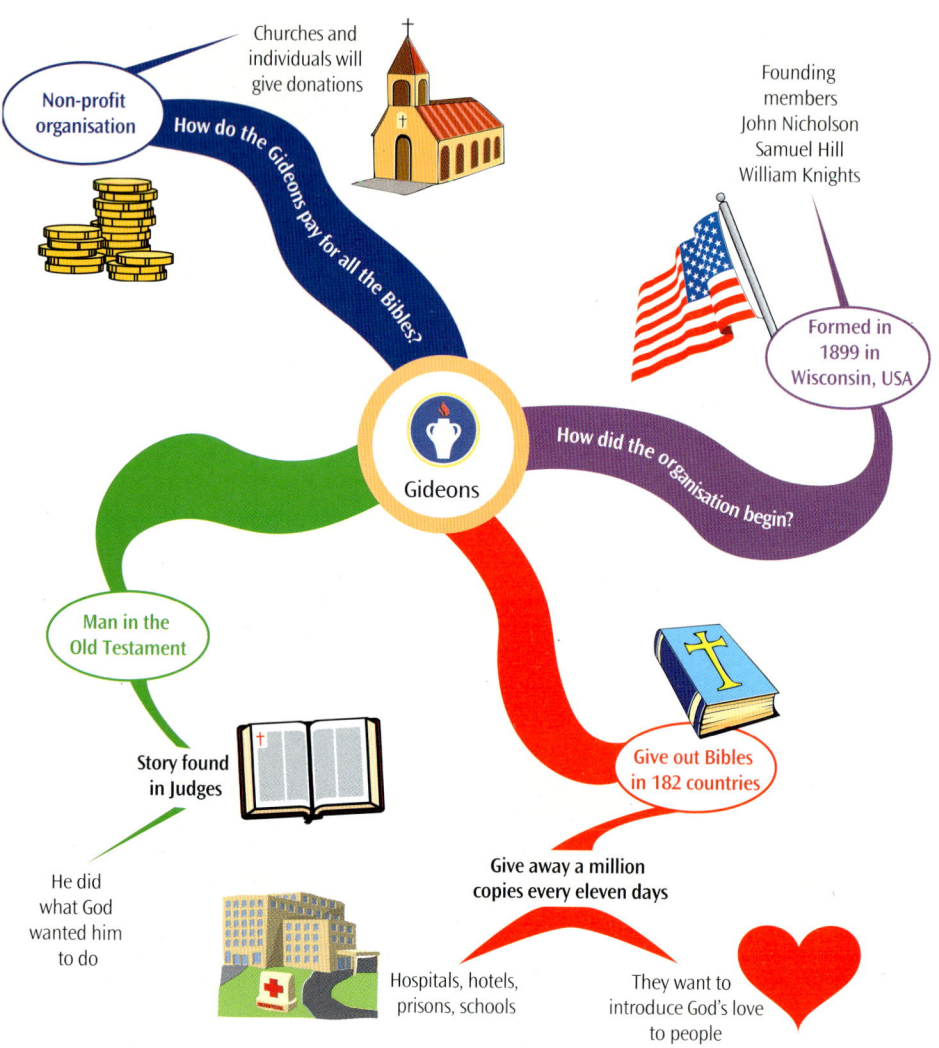

Get Active 3

In groups, choose one of the areas from the mind map to research further. Design a PowerPoint presentation with no more than six slides that explains this area in greater detail. Show and explain your presentation to the rest of your class. The Gideons website will provide you with helpful information (www.gideons.org.uk).

26

2.4 No ordinary book!

Imagine walking into a library. Think about all the books you might find there. Each of these books is very different in style and content and is useful in distinctive ways. For example, you read an encyclopaedia to find out facts, whereas you read Harry Potter for excitement.

The Bible is like a library. It contains many books. These books are very different and can be helpful in various ways.

Inside the Bible

There are two main sections in the Bible – Old Testament and New Testament. The Old Testament records the history of God's chosen people, the Jews. The New Testament records Jesus' life and the beginnings of the Christian Church. The Old Testament was originally written in Hebrew, the language of the Jews, and the New Testament was written in Greek.

The Old Testament is divided into four sections:

▶ **1 Law**
The first five books of the Old Testament are sometimes referred to as the **Pentateuch**. Many people believe that Moses wrote these books. The law books were very important to the Jews as they contain rules about what food they could eat, and how they should behave towards each other and God.

Sample text: Deuteronomy 5: 6–21

▶ **2 History**
The history section records the time when the **Israelites** fought for the land of Israel and settled in it. It describes the lives of their great kings and also many of the bad ones!

Sample text: 1 Samuel 17

> **Information**
>
> **Did you know …**
>
> ▶ … that the longest name in the Bible is Mahershalalhashbaz (Isaiah 8: 1)?
> ▶ … that the Bible is not one book but a collection of 66?
> ▶ … that the Bible has been translated in part or in whole into over 1,200 languages and dialects?
> ▶ … that the Bible is the best-selling book in the world?
> ▶ … that there are two books in the Bible that don't mention God – Song of Solomon and Esther?

Chapter 2 The Bible

▶ **3 Poetry**
The poetry books, like the Psalms, contain songs and poems which would have been used in the synagogue. Some praised and thanked, but others were sad and soul-searching. The Jews also had many proverbs, which applied God's basic common sense to everyday life.

Sample text: Psalm 139: 1–6

▶ **4 Prophets**
There were times when the Israelites did not do what God wanted. God chose men, who became known as prophets, to tell the people that they needed to change their ways. They were sent to the people and even kings to tell them that God was displeased with their behaviour. Prophets came from all sorts of different backgrounds, both rich and poor.

Sample text: Jeremiah 1: 1–10

The New Testament is also divided into four sections:

▶ **1 Gospels**
The first four books of the New Testament are known as **gospels**. The word gospel means 'good news'. Included in the gospels are Jesus' birth, teachings, death, resurrection and ascension.

Sample text: Matthew 26: 47–56

▶ **2 History**
The Acts of the Apostles are an exciting account of the spread of the Christian Church through the Roman Empire. This book tells us a great deal about the lives of the first Christians and the adventures of Peter and Paul.

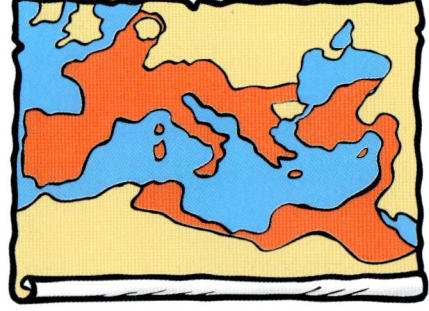

Sample text: Acts 4: 1–4

2.4 No ordinary book!

▶ **3 Letters (Epistles)**

Peter and Paul visited many different towns to tell the people about Jesus. Lots of churches began after their visits, and letters were written to them explaining how to live as a Christian.

Sample text: Colossians 1: 1–6

▶ **4 Prophecy**

The book of Revelation is a series of visions written by John, one of Jesus' disciples. John uses many symbols to describe what he saw. Some of the symbols are easy to understand but many have caused confusion throughout history. Revelation is about God's complete victory over Satan.

Sample text: Revelation 21: 1–5

Get Active 1

Artists throughout history, both Christian and non-Christian, have been so fascinated by the stories of the Bible that they have chosen to illustrate them in their work. Famous examples include Leonardo Da Vinci's *The Last Supper* and Michelangelo's *The Creation of Adam*.

▶ Choose one of the sample texts on pages 27–29. Spend five minutes reading through the text and consider some of the images that it brings to mind.

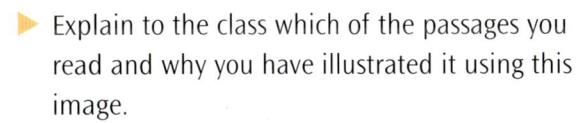

▶ Draw one of these images.

▶ Explain to the class which of the passages you read and why you have illustrated it using this image.

▶ Discuss as a class how effectively you think art communicates the message of the Bible. What do you think are the advantages of churches displaying Bible-inspired art in their buildings? Are there any disadvantages?

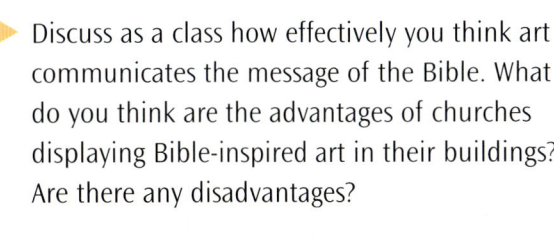

Michelangelo's *The Creation of Adam*

Chapter 2 The Bible

2.5 A love story

Even though the Bible contains many different books of different styles, Christians often talk about the Bible being like one big love story. But why do Christians think of the Bible in this way?

Get Active 1

1 How would you define the word 'love'? How do people express love?

Use the images below to help you think of some ideas. Think of more of your own.

2 How does the idea of 'being loved' make you feel? Think of as many adjectives as possible to describe those feelings, e.g. safe, happy …

The Bible reminds Christians that God loves people – He created them, they are special to Him and He cares about their lives. The love of God is expressed in lots of different ways in both the Old Testament and the New Testament. For example:

▶ **1 Giving**
 God loves His people so much that He wants to give them good things.

▶ **2 Being creative**
 God expresses His love in beautiful words and images – for example, the rainbow is described in the Bible as a sign of God's promises to His people.

2.5 A love story

▶ **3 Comforting**
The Bible describes God as someone we can talk to about our problems, and someone who cares about our lives. One of the books of the Bible, Song of Songs, describes God as like a lover who wants to be intimately involved in the lives of His people.

▶ **4 Jealousy**
In the Bible, God is depicted as a jealous God who does not like it when His people turn away from Him to other things.

▶ **5 Making sacrifices**
Jesus' death on the cross is regarded by Christians to be the most important example of love that anyone has ever made.

Christians are amazed that the mighty and powerful God of all could be interested in the lives of every person, good and bad. It makes them feel special and valued. It causes them to want to offer God their love in return. One book of the Bible, the Psalms, is full of 'love songs' written by people to God.

Here's an example of one such song:

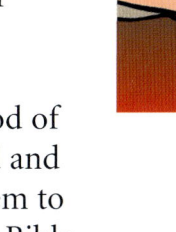

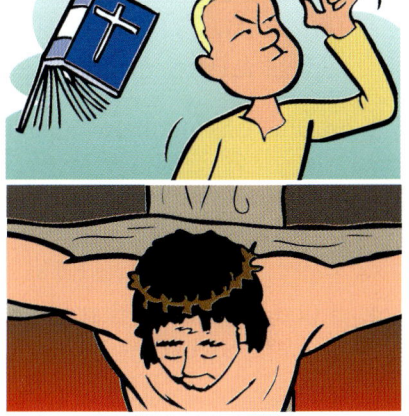

Psalm 103
PSALM OF DAVID

*Praise the L*ORD*, O my soul;*
all my inmost being, praise his holy name.
*Praise the L*ORD*, O my soul, and forget not all his benefits—*
who forgives all your sins
and heals all your diseases,
who redeems your life from the pit
and crowns you with love and compassion,
who satisfies your desires with good things
so that your youth is renewed like the eagle's.

*The L*ORD *works righteousness*
and justice for all the oppressed.

Chapter 2 The Bible

Get Active 2

1. Think of a 'love song' that you are familiar with. In that love song, how does the singer describe their love? What sorts of words and phrases do they use? What things do they praise in the person that they love?

2. Look at David's love song on page 31. How does David describe God's love? What sorts of words and phrases does he use? What things does he praise in God?

3. In what way are the songs you have looked at similar? How do they differ?

Get creative

4. If God is the being that Christians say He is – all-loving, powerful, wise, holy, just, etc. – what sort of love song would *you* write to Him? Try to come up with a verse and chorus that you think would show praise and thankfulness to God.

Summary

The love story of the Bible is one that:

- people are prepared to die for
- people find full of comfort and hope
- the Gideons long for all people to be aware of
- has been accounted for through various authors over hundreds of years.

The Bible: The big task

Having completed the chapter on 'The Bible', complete the following tasks:

1 Listed below are a number of statements about the Bible. Copy and complete the table below. Place the statements into the table based on whether you agree or disagree with them, or are unsure.

   a The Bible is no longer a popular book.

   b The Bible is not relevant to modern life.

   c The Bible has many authors.

   d It is worth making sacrifices to protect the Bible.

   e The Bible is God's word.

   f The Bible is just a rule book.

   g It is very important that the Gideons give Bibles to Year 8s.

   h Only ministers and priests read the Bible.

Agree	Disagree	Unsure

2 Compare your work with your partner's. Circle the statements that you have put in the same columns. Discuss the ones you have disagreed on. Why are your opinions different? Can you change your partner's mind?

Chapter 2 The Bible

3 Check you can do the following:

- Name the two major sections of the Bible.

- Explain two reasons why people think the Bible is special.

- Name an organisation that distributes Bibles.

- Identify three ways Christians believe that God expresses His love.

- Explain what the word 'interpret' means.

- Give one interesting fact about the Bible.

Chapter 3 Relationships – The story of Ruth

Every day we experience and share in different relationships with different people. Look at the diagram below.

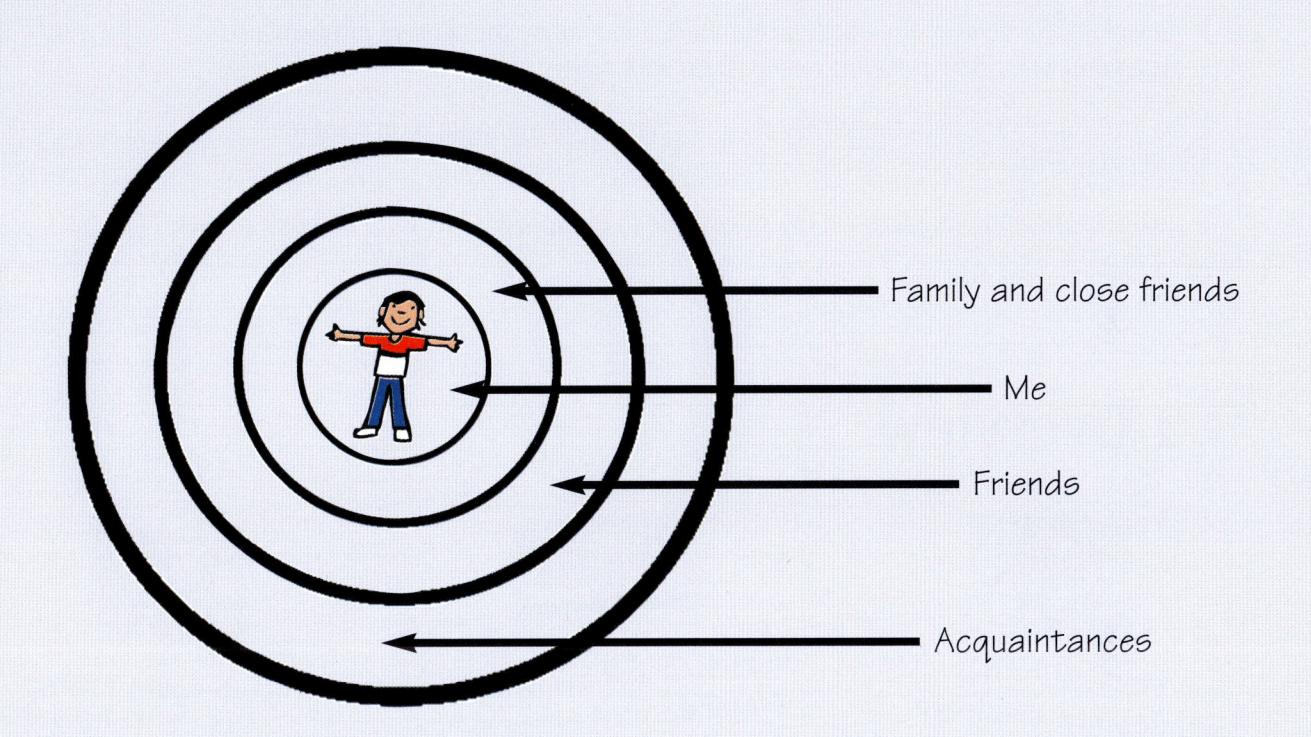

- Family and close friends
- Me
- Friends
- Acquaintances

Copy this diagram onto a blank page. In each section, fill in the names of people in your life that would fall into each of the types of relationship identified above.

Discuss

- ▶ Which circle was easiest to fill in?
- ▶ Which was most difficult?
- ▶ Why do you think that this is the case?
- ▶ How do the relationships you have with each of the groups of people differ?

Chapter 3 Relationships – The story of Ruth

Learning intentions

In this chapter we will be learning:

▶ to explore the story of Ruth

▶ to discover how Ruth chose to be faithful to Naomi and what it means to be **faithful**

▶ to look at examples of the **obedience** of Ruth and analyse the concept of obedience as an important part of having relationships with others

▶ to investigate how Ruth trusted Naomi and consider the importance of **trust** in everyday life

▶ to discuss how the characters in the story chose to love people who were different to them

▶ to identify the emotions a person may experience when they feel like an outsider.

3.1 Overview

1 The story of Ruth is set in a time when Bethlehem was suffering from a great famine.

2 Elimelech and his wife Naomi decided to move their family to Moab, where there was no famine. They took their two sons with them.

3 The family spent many years in Moab. During this time Elimelech died and Naomi's two sons got married. Their wives were called Ruth and Orpah.

4 A number of years later, both boys died, leaving their wives as widows and a grieving mother. Naomi decided that there was nothing left for her in Moab and that it was time for her to move back to Bethlehem.

5 Orpah and Ruth travelled with Naomi, but on the way Naomi told them that they should return home to their families. Orpah did so, but Ruth told Naomi that she would not leave her.

6 Both women returned to Bethlehem. When they arrived there, Ruth decided to start **gleaning** fields in order to provide food for herself and her mother-in-law.

3.1 Overview

7 One of the fields that Ruth worked in belonged to a man called Boaz. Boaz was a relative of Naomi's late husband.

8 Boaz noticed Ruth at work and was kind to her. He made sure that she got enough to eat and that there were extra grains of barley for her to gather in the field.

9 When Ruth told Naomi how kindly she was being treated by Boaz, Naomi had an idea. She encouraged Ruth to dress beautifully the next time she was going to see Boaz. She told Ruth to wait until Boaz lay down to sleep and then to lie down at his feet beside him.

10 When Boaz woke up, Ruth asked him to take her to be his wife. Boaz agreed.

11 Boaz made arrangements for his marriage to Ruth to take place. Boaz had to spend much money and have meetings with the elders of the land before he could get permission to take Ruth as his wife.

12 Boaz and Ruth became husband and wife. Ruth soon became pregnant and she had a son. They called their son Obed. When Obed became a man, he became the father of Jesse, who became the father of David, the king of Israel, from whose line Jesus Christ was born.

Get Active 1

Think of the story of Ruth, in the summary form that you have just read, as the story for a blockbuster movie. Design a poster to advertise the film. Give it an imaginative title and try to come up with a clever tag line. Think of how best to illustrate your poster. In what way could you most dramatically portray the story to ensure that as many people as possible come to watch it?

Chapter 3 Relationships – The story of Ruth

3.2 Faithfulness

Ruth lived in a land called Moab. Elimelech and his family went there to flee the famine in their homeland.

What is a famine?

A **famine** occurs when there is a drastic shortage of food. It can arise as a result of poor weather or a failure of the harvest. There are many accounts of famines occurring throughout the Bible, but this is not simply an ancient crisis. Famines still occur in countries today. Use the internet, or ask your teacher, to list examples of places in which famines are affecting people's lives today.

While Elimelech's family were living in Moab, his sons met two girls – Orpah and Ruth. Orpah married Kilion and Ruth married Machlon. However, after a time Elimelech and his sons died, leaving Naomi, Orpah and Ruth all as widows. Naomi decided that it was time for her to return to her home country, Bethlehem. The famine had ended and her family and friends were there. Naomi urged the girls to return to their families.

Ruth, however, refused to leave Naomi. She said:

> *Don't urge me to leave you or to turn back from you. Where you go I will go, and where you stay I will stay. Your people will be my people and your God my God. Where you die I will die, and there I will be buried. May the LORD deal with me, be it ever so severely, if anything but death separates you and me.*
> **RUTH 1: 16–17**

Ruth was faithful to Naomi, even though it meant she had to leave her homeland, and move to a new place where she would be a stranger. It must have taken great love, courage and faith for Ruth to make the choice she did.

3.2 Faithfulness

Get Active 1

Complete the following tasks:

1. Draw a family tree that represents the family at the centre of this story.
2. Write a brief account of the reasons why Naomi decided she wanted to return to Bethlehem.
3. Rewrite Ruth's words to Naomi in modern English.

Sometimes being faithful to others, or being faithful to what we know is right, means that we, like Ruth, need to leave our place of comfort and risk being looked on as different.

What do we mean when we describe someone as being faithful?

For example, consider the following situation:

In your youth club, there is one person who is always left out and is laughed at by the others. This person is not as good as others at sport and dresses in very old-fashioned clothes. People often say things behind this person's back. They call this person 'ugly', or 'fat', or 'stupid'. Some of the boys even say that everyone should avoid this person so that they don't return to the group. Some don't want to talk to this person, but don't want them to leave the group either, because then there wouldn't be anyone to make fun of.

▶ What is the easiest way to respond to this situation?

▶ What is the kindest way to deal with this situation?

▶ Why is the kindest way the most difficult?

▶ Why is it hard being different from other people?

Now complete the activity on the following page.

Chapter 3 Relationships – The story of Ruth

Get Active 2

1 First, copy and complete the following chart on the basis of the youth club story you have just read on page 39.

Situation:			
Outline the situation in three bullet points.			
▶			
▶			
▶			
Possible solution 1:		Possible solution 2:	
Advantages	Disadvantages	Advantages	Disadvantages

2 Then, complete a similar chart for Ruth when she was told by Naomi to return to her family.

3.3 Trust

One of the most famous tightrope walkers of all time was a man who called himself Blondin. Many people went to admire his performances. One of his favourite shows was to walk across Niagara Falls to demonstrate his amazing ability. Reportedly, on one occasion when giving one of these shows a man in front yelled out to him, 'You are the greatest tightrope walker in the world!' Blondin looked at the man and asked, 'Do you really think so? Do you think I could walk across that cable pushing a wheelbarrow?' The man replied, 'Yes, I believe you could!' Blondin amazed the crowd by pushing the wheelbarrow across the Falls and back. The crowd cheered and the man shouted, 'I knew you could do it since you are the greatest in the world!' Blondin smiled at the man and asked, 'Do you think I could push this wheelbarrow across the falls with 150 pounds of weight in it?' The man replied, 'Yes, I certainly believe you could!' Blondin then looked at the man and said, 'All right. Climb in!'

Do you think you would have had the courage to climb into the wheelbarrow? To do so would require an awful lot of faith in the tightrope walker.

Faith is important in our everyday lives. Think about the following situations. In what way is faith important in each one?

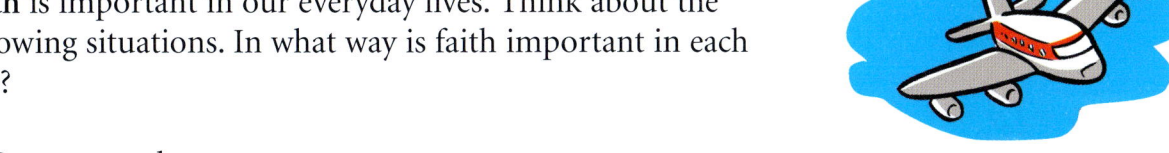

▶ On an aeroplane
▶ Asking for directions in a new school
▶ Telling a friend a secret
▶ Appointing a prime minister

Chapter 3 Relationships – The story of Ruth

Get Active 1

1. In pairs, think about a situation in which you have had to trust someone else and have found it easy to do so. Share the situation with your partner.

2. Imagine another situation in which you have had to trust someone else and have found this very difficult.

3. Compare the situations. Why was it easier to trust in one situation than in the other? Why are some people easier to trust than others?

In the story of Ruth, we find Ruth having to **trust** and obey Naomi's instructions.

Here's what Naomi says to Ruth:

> My dear daughter, isn't it about time I arranged a good home for you so you can have a happy life? And isn't Boaz, our close relative, the one with whose young women you've been working? Maybe it's time to make our move. Tonight is the night of Boaz's barley harvest at the threshing floor. Take a bath. Put on some perfume. Get all dressed up and go to the threshing floor. But don't let him know you're there until the party is well under way and he's had plenty of food and drink. When you see him slipping off to sleep, watch where he lies down and then go there. Lie at his feet to let him know that you are available to him for marriage. Then wait and see what he says. He'll tell you what to do.

Naomi's instructions must have seemed strange to Ruth. Ruth must have felt very nervous about carrying them out. However, she trusted Naomi and did as she was told to do. In the end, Boaz took Ruth as his wife and looked after her as Naomi had said he would.

Christians believe that, even though some of the instructions in the Bible may seem strange or difficult to carry out, following them is for our own good. Christians believe it is important to trust God and obey Him even when it is difficult to do so.

Here are some examples of instructions or rules that are found in the Bible that may seem a little odd.

- Honour your parents.
- Love your enemies.
- Do not get angry.

Why might these commandments make our society a better place? Why is it hard to carry out each of them?

Christians believe that God is responsible for the creation of the world, and therefore He understands best how it should work. Therefore His instructions are worth trusting in and obeying.

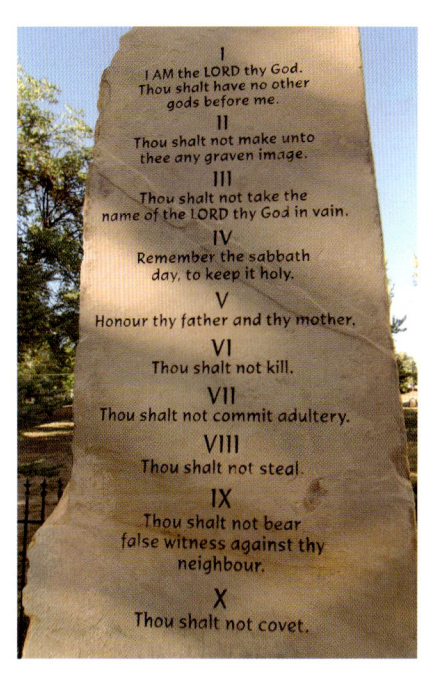

The Ten Commandments

Get Active 2

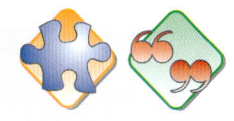

Imagine that you are taking part in a chat show. Each person in your group must take on the persona of one of the characters from the story: Naomi, Ruth, Boaz, field worker, chat show host.

You will be given fifteen minutes to plan some of the questions that each of the characters should be asked. Practise dramatising your chat show. Perform your drama in front of the rest of the class.

Chapter 3 Relationships – The story of Ruth

3.4 Loving those who are different

At the time of the story of Ruth, the Jews were often intolerant of outsiders. Many of them believed that friendships and relationships with those who were not of their faith were to be avoided. They had several reasons for this:

- 1 They believed that this would ensure that Jews were not tempted to follow other religions.
- 2 They believed that this would help to make sure that Jews were not tempted to do things that the law of God did not allow.
- 3 The Jews believed that they were God's chosen people and that other people had rejected God's goodness, and therefore were sinners to be avoided.

However, the story of Ruth is a story in which outsiders are treated with love and compassion. Let's look at some examples:

- Naomi's sons marry women who are Moabites. Moabites worshipped many different gods. As part of their faith they performed human sacrifices. The Jews would have totally disagreed with the Moabite faith, and yet Naomi's sons accepted and loved these girls.
- When Naomi's sons died, Naomi remained kind and loving in her treatment of her daughters-in-law.
- When Ruth's husband dies, she loves Naomi nonetheless and pledges her loyalty to her. The book that contains this story even suggests that Ruth took on the Jewish religion.
- Boaz treats Ruth, a foreigner to his land, with kindness and eventually marries her.

The story of Ruth is, therefore, a story of love for the outsider, love for those rejected by others and love for those deemed unlovable. The story reminds us of the importance of loving other people and treating them with value despite their background, gender, religion or race.

3.4 Loving those who are different

Get Active 1

1 Answer the following questions:

▶ What do you know about the religion of the Moabites?

▶ Write in your book one example of love being shown to someone who is different in the story of Ruth.

▶ How do you think it made Ruth feel when Naomi and Boaz treated her with kindness?

Think of one question of your own that you would like to ask the teacher about the story.

2 There are many people in our society who feel like outsiders and are often treated like outsiders. Can you think of examples of groups of people who may be treated in this way? Why are each of these groups disliked?

Very often the reason we are quick to criticise people and treat them like outsiders is because they are different from us. It is important to remind ourselves that the world is a better and more interesting place because it contains such a variety of people. Imagine the world being full of people who are exactly like you; think how the world would miss out, or be less interesting if that were so.

Christians also believe that it is important to consider that God loves all people, despite how they behave, where they are from, who they are. So it is important for us to do the same.

It is also worth remembering that it is easy to criticise others if we haven't put ourselves in their shoes. Whenever we begin to think about how our actions affect others, it can often discourage us from continuing to behave in the way we have done.

There are many situations in which we can feel like outsiders. Can you think of some examples?

Chapter 3 Relationships – The story of Ruth

Get Active 2

Look at the following acrostic (where the first letter of each line makes up the word 'Outsider'):

On my own again,
Unloved, unwanted
Trying to understand why I'm
So often taunted.
Inside I'm crying,
Don't want others to see
Every day their harsh words
Really hurt me.

This is a poem written to express the hurt felt by a young person who is treated like an outsider. Try to put yourself in the shoes of someone who feels like this. Write an acrostic of your own. It doesn't have to rhyme. Focus on using words that particularly describe *feelings* and *emotions*.

Conclusion

The story of Ruth is a story about faithfulness, obedience and loving kindness:

- Naomi is kind to Ruth – gives her blessing for her to return home.
- Ruth is kind to Naomi – sticking by her and providing for her.
- Boaz is kind to Ruth – accepting and loving her.
- God is kind to His people.

Each of the main characters in the story goes beyond the call of duty to help others. The result of the loving kindness shown between them is a group of people who support and care for each other.

3.4 Loving those who are different

The Jewish word for this loving kindness is **Hesed**. Hesed continues to be an important part of the Jewish understanding of how we should treat people today. Christians also stress the importance of treating others in this same way.

In the story of Ruth, God is seen as looking after those who are faithful to Him. Jews and Christians continue to believe that, if we perform acts of Hesed in our lives, God will look after us and be faithful to us.

Are there ways in which we can show such kindness in our own lives?

Summary

Ruth is the story of a woman who:

- ▶ was faithful to her mother-in-law, Naomi
- ▶ trusted Naomi even when Naomi asked her to do things that were difficult
- ▶ loved those from whom she was different, and was loved by these people in return
- ▶ demonstrated loving kindness in her relationships with others.

Ruth and Naomi in Boaz's field

Chapter 3 Relationships – The story of Ruth

The story of Ruth: The big task

Having completed the chapter on 'The story of Ruth', complete the following task:

'The story of Ruth contains messages that are relevant for life in the twenty-first century.' Do you think there is evidence to support this statement?

Use the knowledge and understanding that you have gained from this chapter to write a short essay in answer to the question. Try to express a personal opinion based on evidence: you could decide that the messages of the story are different from those suggested in this chapter, so long as you provide evidence for your opinions.

Use the following table to help you think about what to include in your answer and to ensure your response is as detailed as possible.

As evidence for this statement	Completed ✓/✗
I can mention at least **three** characters from the story of Ruth.	
I can quote at least **two** incidents from the life of Ruth.	
I understand that both Jews and Christians believe that this story teaches them about God and how to treat others.	
I can give an opinion on the relevance of the story of Ruth for life today, which I include in the conclusion.	
I can justify my opinion by giving at least **two** reasons for it.	

Once you have completed your answer, swap it with a partner, and ensure that you can tick each row in the table for their work. If not, advise your partner how they could improve their work. Make any changes you need to make to your own work before handing it in for your teacher to mark.

Chapter 4
Who is Jesus?

In 2004, Kanye West released the single 'Jesus Walks'. The lyrics speak of the artist's need for Jesus in his life. He compares it to the way in which each school needs teachers. The song describes God's faithfulness – Jesus hears his prayers, He shows him the way and, above, all, He walks with him in all circumstances. When he has things wrong in his life, Jesus still walks with him. When he hasn't spoken to God in ages, Jesus still walks with him. He also sings of how Jesus walks with each person, even with murderers or drug dealers.

Kanye West

Jesus, a man who walked the earth over 2000 years ago, is also an individual who continues to attract attention among people today. This attention is not simply confined to members of the Christian Church. Jesus' life is one that fascinates pop stars, artists, actors, film directors, authors, old people, young people, the rich, the poor.

One website that is dedicated to the life of Jesus is 'rejesus'. Go to www.rejesus.co.uk/encounters/quote_unquote/index.html.

Look through the different things that individuals, past and present, have said about Jesus. Pick one quotation that you find particularly appealing. Write it into your classwork book. Then complete the sentence: I find this quotation interesting because …

Share your sentences as a class. Discuss the points that others make.

Chapter 4 Who is Jesus?

Learning intentions

In this chapter we will be learning:

- ▶ the details of the story of the birth of Jesus
- ▶ to consider Jesus' mission to change the world
- ▶ to examine the characters of the men Jesus chose as his disciples
- ▶ to look at examples of Jesus' power in action
- ▶ why Jesus was put to death
- ▶ to consider Jesus as a role model and his significance for people today.

4.1 Introduction

'Google' the name of our Queen and you're likely to get over 3 million results displayed. Try it for David Beckham – he'll get more than 7 million. George Bush gains over 88 million results. Then try it for Jesus – and you'll discover over 120 million references.

It is clear that Jesus is popular with many people. But why? What is it about Jesus – a man born over 2000 years ago, who travelled little, who was not rich or influential – that interests so many people in the world?

Get Active 1

In groups, create a spider diagram that shows the words and phrases that come to your minds when you think of Jesus. Consider what you think he might have looked like. Think about what sort of person he might have been. What ideas do you come up with?

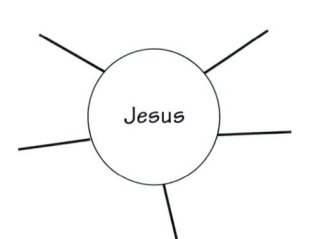

4.1 Introduction

Often when people think of Jesus, the picture that comes to mind is of him lying as a quiet baby in a stable. However, many people who have read the stories of Jesus' life contained in the Bible have seen him to be much more than simply the child that does not cry.

Some have seen him as a revolutionary.

Some have seen him as a radical monk.

Some have seen him as a holy prophet.

Some have viewed him as a trouble maker.

Some, as a man who suffered.

Perhaps, beyond our 'Christmas card' image of Jesus, there is much more to him than has previously met the eye.

51

Chapter 4 Who is Jesus?

4.2 Unique birth

Think about a situation in which someone you know has been expecting a baby. Everyone gets very excited about the child that is going to be born. There are often preparations made for the baby's arrival.

When Princess Diana was pregnant with her first child, the whole country was filled with that sense of excitement, for the child to be born would be in line to the throne. When Prince William was eventually born, the news was immediately spread through television, radio and newspapers. Important people from all around the world sent gifts and good wishes to the newborn child and his parents.

Princess Diana with Prince William

Jesus is often referred to by Christians as the 'King of Kings' and the 'Prince of Peace', yet his 'royal birth' was uniquely different to the birth of most royal children. It was without publicity, glamour or even comfort.

Here are some of the key details of Jesus' birth:

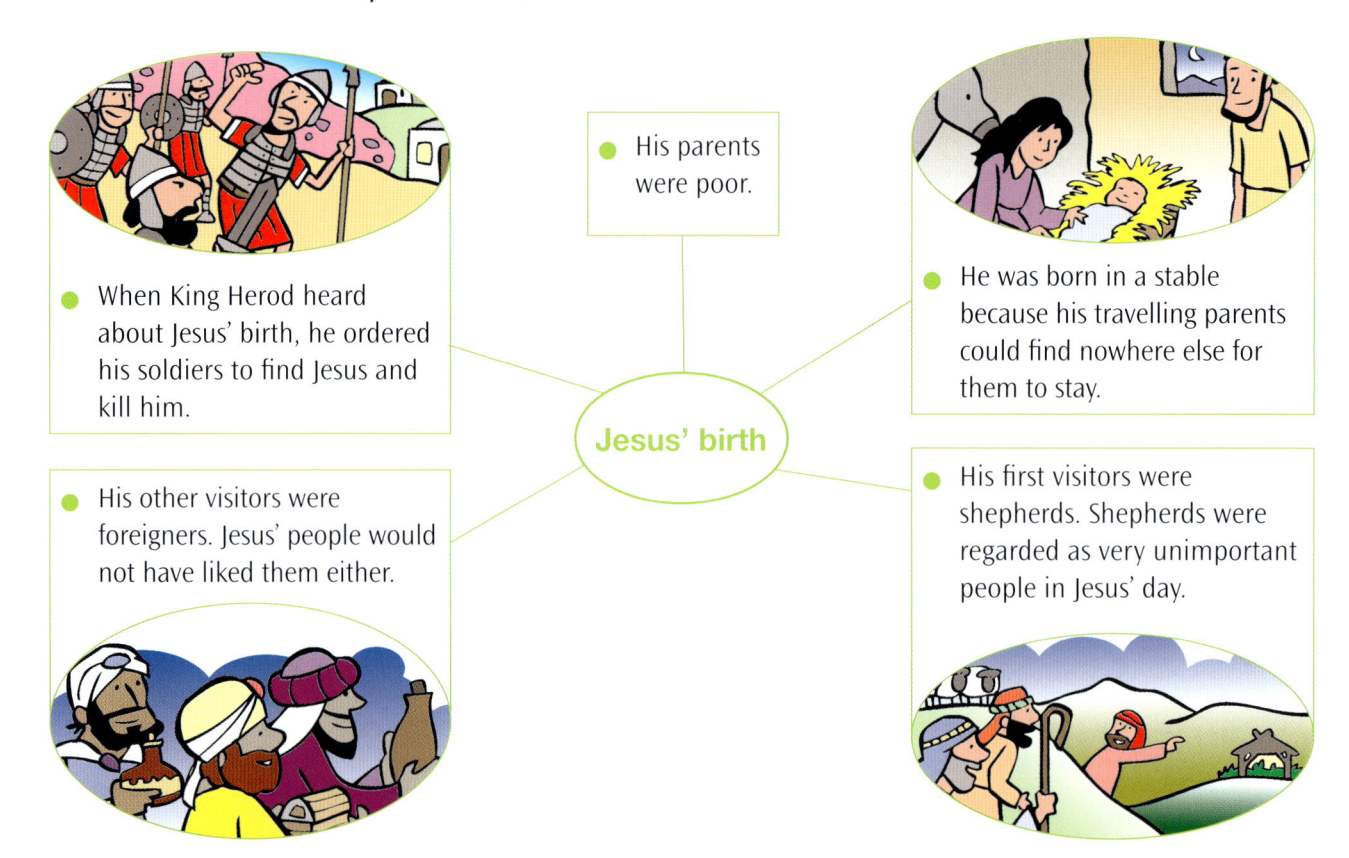

- When King Herod heard about Jesus' birth, he ordered his soldiers to find Jesus and kill him.

- His parents were poor.

- He was born in a stable because his travelling parents could find nowhere else for them to stay.

Jesus' birth

- His other visitors were foreigners. Jesus' people would not have liked them either.

- His first visitors were shepherds. Shepherds were regarded as very unimportant people in Jesus' day.

4.2 Unique birth

Get Active 1

In pairs, try to compose a news update announcing the birth of Jesus. Emphasise that Jesus' birth is unique.

Use the Biblical accounts of the story of Jesus' birth to help you. These are found in Matthew 1: 18 to 2: 18 and Luke 2: 1–20.

The story of Jesus' birth is clearly unique. As we look back on Jesus' birth, knowing his significance for people today, the details are unexpected. Yet an even more amazing aspect to Jesus' birth is that it had been predicted many hundreds of years before it actually happened!

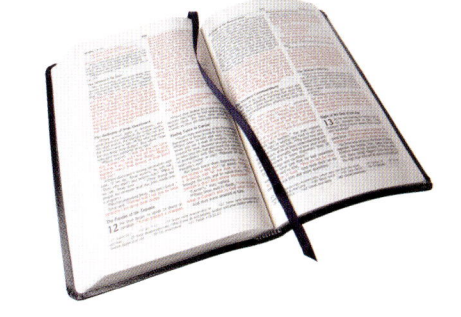

Look at these three passages:

MICAH 5: 2
But you, Bethlehem, though you are small among the clans of Judah, out of you will come for me one who will be ruler over Israel, whose origins are from of old, from ancient times.

ISAIAH 9: 6
For to us a child is born, to us a son is given, and the government will be on his shoulders. And he will be called Wonderful Counsellor, Mighty God, Everlasting Father, Prince of Peace.

ISAIAH 7: 14
Therefore the Lord himself will give you a sign: The virgin will be with child and will give birth to a son, and will call him Immanuel.

In total, more than 300 prophecies like these were made in the Old Testament that relate to Jesus' life, death and resurrection. This makes his birth very unique.

Get Active 2

Christians believe that Jesus' birth was planned by God from the beginning of time, and that Jesus came to Earth to tell people of God's love. The central message of Christmas, the celebration of Jesus' birth, is a message of hope and love.

In groups, think of a person or group of people who might feel unloved and hopeless. Devise an action plan for how you could demonstrate by your actions the Christian message of love and hope to them.

Chapter 4 Who is Jesus?

4.3 Unique mission

When Jesus began his ministry, he said that he had come to fulfil an important mission. Jesus sought, throughout his life, to complete this mission. In the synagogue at Nazareth, Jesus said that he had come to do three things, and here are some examples of how he went about it:

Preach good news to the poor

- Jesus said 'Blessed are the poor'.
- Jesus associated with those who had little wealth.
- Jesus picked disciples who were poor as well as some who were rich.

Give sight to the blind

- Jesus healed many sick people, including a number who were blind. One particularly well-known example of this is when Jesus healed blind Bartimaeus.

Bring freedom to prisoners

- Christians believe that Jesus died in order that people can have their sins forgiven. Christians believe that Jesus took punishment for them, on their behalf.

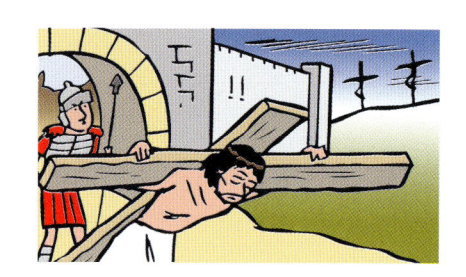

Jesus had concern for social issues. He wanted the world to be a better place. He wanted people to be treated more fairly. He wanted communities to know that God cared for them.

Christians see Jesus as their example or role model. Many Christians try to follow Jesus' example by being concerned about the same issues that Jesus was concerned with.

4.3 Unique mission

Get Active 1

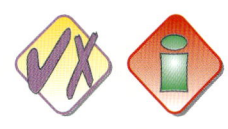

Choose one of the following Christian organisations and use the internet, or information provided by your teacher, to construct a poster that advertises the work they do.

- Preaching good news – **Trócaire**

- Helping the most vulnerable – **CBM**

- Campaigning for freedom for captives – **Release International**

Jesus' mission was to change people's lives – and to set an example for how people should live. Jesus is a role model for Christian people.

We, too, can be role models for others. The example we set can be a positive one or a negative one.

Think about who looks up to you and who you have an influence on. Younger family members? Friends? Members of organisations you are involved in?

Get Active 2

Discuss the following questions:

1. Can you identify a person you think of as a good role model?
2. What makes this individual, or any individual, a good role model?
3. What sort of person would be a bad role model?
4. Can you think of any specific examples of famous individuals who could be described as bad role models?

Chapter 4 Who is Jesus?

4.4 Unique followers

Imagine you are picking a team (football, netball, hockey, rugby): what sort of people will you choose? What are the 'essential skills' you are looking for? Will all the players be good at the same things? Will they all have similar skills? If so, why? If not, why not? Remember that the aim of your team is to try to win games. You want to pick the players who will best help you do this.

Jesus, in trying to fulfil his mission, had to pick a team of people to help him. Here's who he picked:

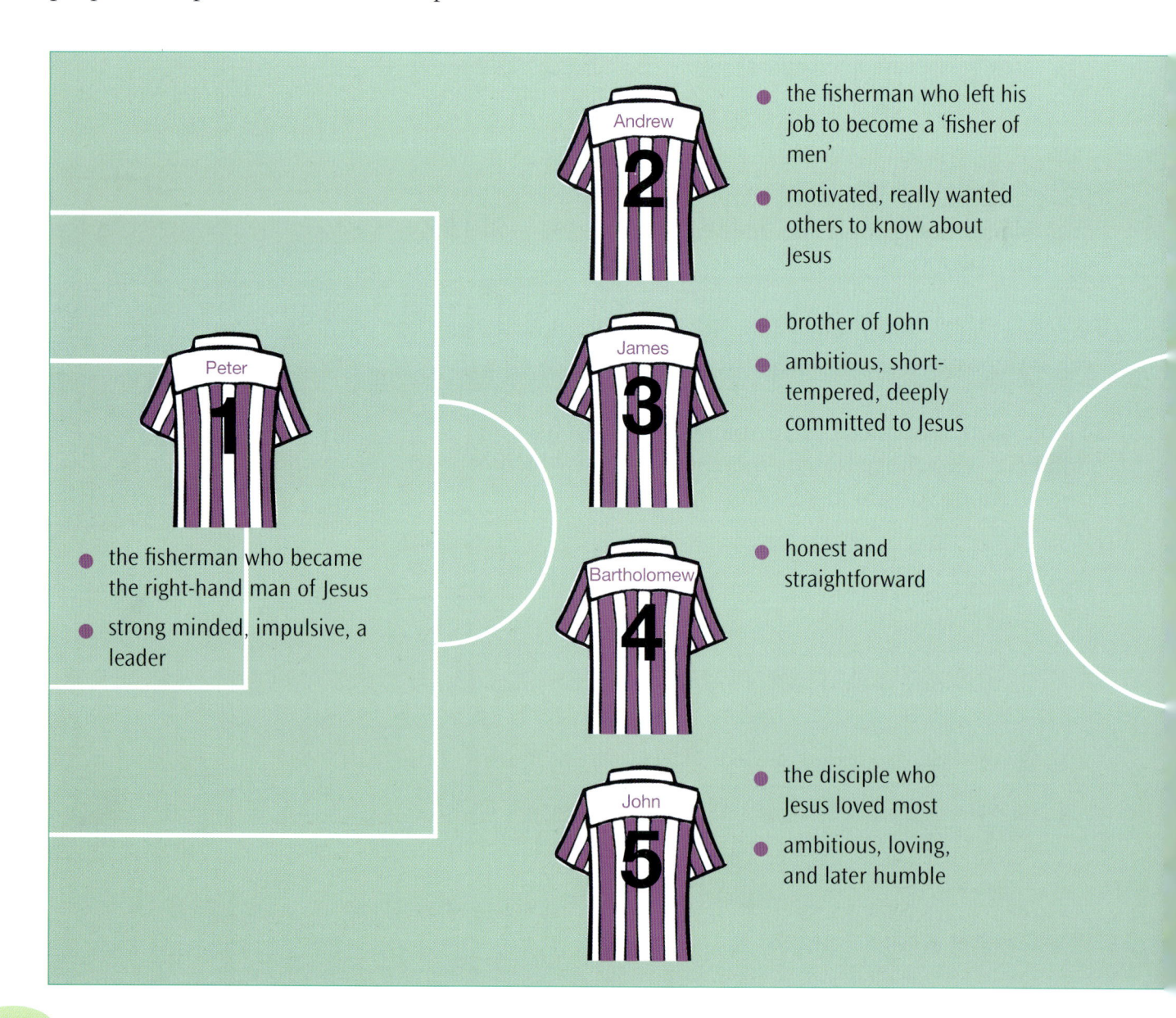

Peter (1)
- the fisherman who became the right-hand man of Jesus
- strong minded, impulsive, a leader

Andrew (2)
- the fisherman who left his job to become a 'fisher of men'
- motivated, really wanted others to know about Jesus

James (3)
- brother of John
- ambitious, short-tempered, deeply committed to Jesus

Bartholomew (4)
- honest and straightforward

John (5)
- the disciple who Jesus loved most
- ambitious, loving, and later humble

4.4 Unique followers

Get Active 1

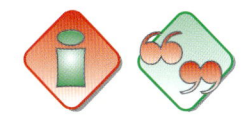

Discuss in pairs:

1. What do you think would be the 'essential skills' needed to be a follower of Jesus and to help him fulfil his mission? List your answers.

2. Compare your results with the rest of the class. Decide which characteristics would be most essential.

Sub's bench

Judas — 12
- supported Jesus only for a short time
- later was greedy and became a traitor

Matthew — 6
- tax collector
- is believed to have written the gospel of Matthew

Philip — 7
- fisherman
- liked to ask questions

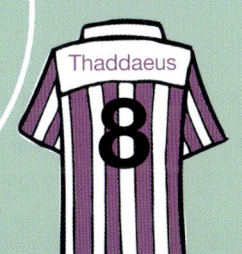

Thaddaeus — 8
- little is known about Thaddaeus
- he became a missionary after Jesus' death

Thomas — 9
- full of courage
- sometimes doubted – liked things to be proven before he could believe them to be true

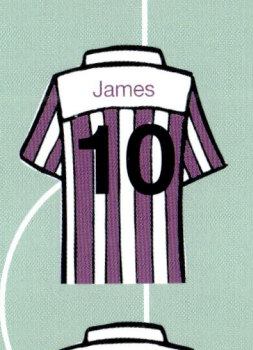

James — 10
- a patriot
- loved his nation

Simon — 11
- a fisherman
- had strong political views

Chapter 4 Who is Jesus?

Peter – the team captain

Peter's life went something like this:

- He worked as a fisherman.
- He was called by Jesus and became a disciple.
- Jesus called him 'a rock'.
- He pretended not to know Jesus when Jesus was arrested.
- When Jesus rose from the dead, he forgave Peter and asked him to go out and tell others about him.
- He was eventually killed on account of his faith.

Peter was pointed out as special by Jesus because he didn't just believe the same as everyone else around him. He saw something special about Jesus and wasn't scared to say this even though others might disagree with him.

Get Active 2

1. Think of four issues that people might disagree on. Put the issue in the form of a statement, for example 'I believe that smoking is wrong'.

2. The teacher will choose some of these issues on which you can have a class debate. Try the 'four corner' method of debate. Each corner of the room will represent agree, disagree, strongly agree, or strongly disagree. Stand in the corner that most closely represents your opinion on the issue. Be prepared to justify your view if the teacher asks! Can you convince others to move from their corner to yours?

4.5 Unique power

Throughout his ministry, Jesus spoke many wise words. He said things that were controversial too. For example, he said that the poor were blessed – in other words, that they were especially favoured by God. This was difficult for some of the people around Jesus to accept. They thought that having money was a sign that God was pleased with you.

Jesus, however, didn't just say things that surprised people. He also did surprising and unique things too. Jesus became known by the people around him as a miracle worker. Indeed, if we read the gospel books, we find a miracle recorded on almost every page.

But, where did Jesus' unique power come from? And what did he use this unique power for?

Where did Jesus' power come from?

Read the story opposite, taken from the gospel of Mark. This story takes place after Jesus is recorded as having driven evil spirits out of a possessed man.

MARK 3: 22–26
The teachers of the law who came down from Jerusalem said [about Jesus], 'He is possessed by Beelzebub [the devil]! It is the chief of the demons who gives him the power to drive them out.' So Jesus called them and spoke to them in parables: 'How can Satan drive out Satan? If a country divides itself into groups that fight each other, that country will fall apart. If a family divides itself into groups that fight each other, that family will fall apart. And if Satan's kingdom divides into groups, it cannot last, but will fall apart and come to an end.'

Get Active 1

Think about the images that Jesus uses in responding to the teachers of the Law in the Bible quote:

▶ A country dividing and fighting within itself.

▶ A family dividing and being in conflict.

It is easy to understand the point made in each image – if a group of people begin to fight within themselves, that group will fall apart.

What, therefore, does Jesus mean when he talks about Satan's kingdom dividing into groups? Why does he use this illustration to defend himself?

Chapter 4 Who is Jesus?

What does Jesus use his power for?

Jesus never used miracles to show off or to help himself. In fact, often he asked those he had healed not to tell anyone what he had done.

Jesus used miracles to:

- 1 strengthen people's faith
- 2 show God's power
- 3 help people.

The miracles that Jesus performed took different forms, including healing, changing the weather and raising the dead.

Get Active 2

Read Luke 8: 40–56 on the next page.

1 Jesus performs two miracles in this passage; what are they?

2 With the help of your teacher, unpack this story.

Try to find out:

- what the woman did to be healed
- what effect this had on Jesus
- what Jesus said had healed her
- what Jesus said Jairus had to do in order for his daughter to be well
- what Jesus did to make her well.

3 Imagine what it would have been like to have witnessed one of these events taking place. How do you think you would have felt? Amazed? Shocked? Scared?

4.5 Unique power

LUKE 8: 40–56

Now when Jesus returned, a crowd welcomed him, for they were all expecting him. Then a man named Jairus, a ruler of the synagogue, came and fell at Jesus' feet, pleading with him to come to his house because his only daughter, a girl of about twelve, was dying. As Jesus was on his way, the crowds almost crushed him. And a woman was there who had been subject to bleeding for twelve years, but no one could heal her. She came up behind him and touched the edge of his cloak, and immediately her bleeding stopped. 'Who touched me?' Jesus asked. When they all denied it, Peter said, 'Master, the people are crowding and pressing against you.' But Jesus said, 'Someone touched me; I know that power has gone out from me.' Then the woman, seeing that she could not go unnoticed, came trembling and fell at his feet. In the presence of all the people, she told why she had touched him and how she had been instantly healed. Then he said to her, 'Daughter, your faith has healed you. Go in peace.' While Jesus was still speaking, someone came from the house of Jairus, the synagogue ruler. 'Your daughter is dead,' he said. 'Don't bother the teacher any more.' Hearing this, Jesus said to Jairus, 'Don't be afraid; just believe, and she will be healed.' When he arrived at the house of Jairus, he did not let anyone go in with him except Peter, John and James, and the child's father and mother. Meanwhile, all the people were wailing and mourning for her. 'Stop wailing,' Jesus said. 'She is not dead but asleep.' They laughed at him, knowing that she was dead. But he took her by the hand and said, 'My child, get up!' Her spirit returned, and at once she stood up. Then Jesus told them to give her something to eat. Her parents were astonished, but he ordered them not to tell anyone what had happened.

Many of the people who witnessed the miracles of Jesus were unsure about how to feel about what he had done. Some thought that Jesus' miracles showed that he was a man of God. Some thought that Jesus' miracles were performed using evil powers. Some were scared when Jesus did great miracles before them. Some were totally confused by them.

Get Active 3

Hot seat: Jesus and a disciple

In groups, prepare five questions you would ask Jesus or one of his disciples about the miracles you have studied. Also prepare the answers you would give if you were Jesus or the disciple.

Get one person from the class to volunteer to be Jesus and one to volunteer to be the disciple. Each group asks one of their questions to them. This continues until all the questions have been asked. The class then discusses the answers that Jesus and the disciple gave, and whether they would agree with them.

Chapter 4 Who is Jesus?

4.6 Unique death

Have you ever read *The Lion, the Witch and the Wardrobe*, or seen the film? Here's a very famous section of the story in which Aslan allows himself to be put to death to save the life of Edmund:

When once Aslan had been tied on the flat stone, a hush fell on the crowd. Four Hags, holding four torches, stood at the corners of the Table. The Witch bared her arms as she had bared them the previous night when it had been Edmund instead of Aslan. Then she began to whet her knife …

At last she drew near. She stood by Aslan's head. Her face was working and twitching with passion, but his looked up at the sky, still quiet, neither angry nor afraid, but a little sad. Then, just before she gave the blow, she stooped down and said in a quivering voice,

'And now, who has won? Fool, did you think that by all this you would save the human traitor? Now I will kill you instead of him as our pact was and so the Deep Magic will be appeased …'

C.S. Lewis, The Lion, the Witch and the Wardrobe

When we read the story, we find it incredible that Aslan does not fight back against the wicked queen. Aslan, throughout the story, has shown himself to be full of power – he is the most powerful in the land – and yet he does not defend himself. He allows those around him to put him to death so that Edmund might go free.

Get Active 1

Aslan sacrificed his life for Edmund. In our world, there are many men and women who are prepared to sacrifice themselves for the safety and freedom of others. For example, think of all the policemen, firemen and ambulance men who lost their lives trying to rescue individuals from the Twin Towers on 11 September.

1 Create 'mood' boards: consider the themes 'sacrifice', 'loss' and 'national pride and honour'.

In groups, create a large collage that represents each of the themes using newspaper cuttings, images, words and drawings. Think about the use of colour and shape in creating the 'mood' of each theme. The mood board should be created to convey the emotion of each theme as well as examples of each in action and the opinions of others.

2 Look at the work the other groups have completed. Discuss the particular images or words that especially convey the themes to you.

4.6 Unique death

C.S. Lewis, author of *The Lion, the Witch and the Wardrobe*, was a Christian writer. He wrote the story of Aslan's death as a way of helping young people to think about the death of Jesus.

We have discovered previously that Jesus was a man of significant power. He could do many exceptional things. Yet when some of the leaders of his land turned against him, Jesus did not run away or fight back. Like Aslan, he was prepared to face death.

Christians believe that, just as Aslan died to save Edmund, Jesus died to save humans. Perhaps you're wondering what humans need to be saved from? Christians believe that Jesus came to save humans from the power of sin, death and meaninglessness.

Jesus said that he 'did not come to be served; he came to serve, and to give his life to redeem many people' (Mark 10: 45).

Is there anything that you would be prepared to sacrifice in order to 'save' others?

Get Active 2

Many people in our world live in desperate poverty. Do we have a responsibility to help them? Should young people be doing more to help them? Check out the 'Buy Nothing Christmas' campaign: www.buynothingchristmas.org.

This is a movement that challenges individuals to think less about buying presents at Christmas, and more about giving to others. Do you think this is a good idea? Would you be interested in being involved in a campaign like this? If so, why? If not, why not?

HAVE LESS LIVE MORE

WWW.BUYNOTHINGCHRISTMAS.ORG

Chapter 4 Who is Jesus?

Summary

Jesus was a unique man whose life was extraordinary in many ways. He had:

- a unique birth in Bethlehem that had been foretold many years before
- a unique mission which involved preaching good news to the poor, giving sight to the blind and freeing prisoners
- a unique set of followers, one of the most important being Peter
- unique power with which he sought to help those around him
- a unique death that Christians believe provides them with salvation for their sins.

Who is Jesus? The big task

Having completed the chapter on 'Who is Jesus?', complete the following task:

Working in groups, use recycled materials to create a sculpture that reflects the uniqueness of Jesus. Think carefully about how you would portray the different aspects of Jesus' life that have been addressed in this chapter. It is not the sculpture itself that is important but the explanation given. Once the sculpture is completed each group will explain to the rest of the class the symbolism of their work.

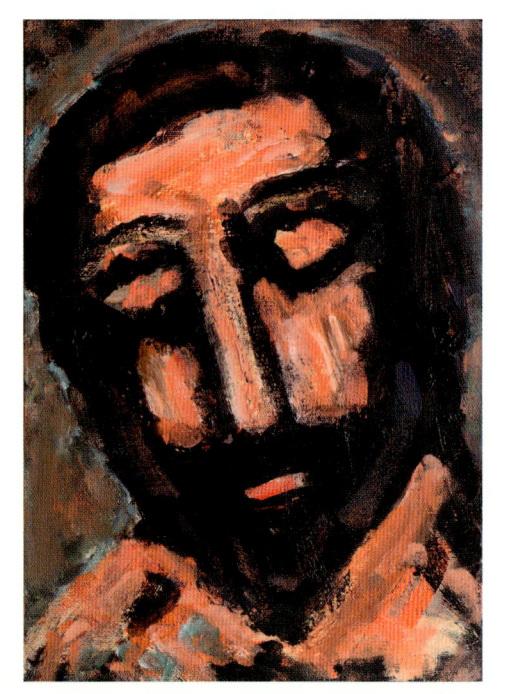

Or

Draw a portrait of Jesus that reflects his uniqueness. Be as creative as possible. Try to include symbols, colours and images that would portray the uniqueness of Jesus. Include many of the themes and ideas addressed in this chapter. Think back to the research you completed into different artists' paintings of Jesus. Use these to inspire your portrait. Once you have completed your portrait show it to the class and explain its meaning.

An oil painting of Jesus

Chapter 5
The Christian Church

Making 'sense' of it!

Imagine walking into this church building. What sort of experience would that be?

To help you think about this, consider your five senses.

Discuss

- What kinds of sounds do you think that you would *hear*? Would the building be noisy or quiet?
- What different things do you think you would *see* around you?
- Would this place have a distinctive *smell*? What would it smell like?
- How would the place '*feel*'? What do you think the temperature would be like? Describe how you think some of the furnishings might feel if you were to touch them.
- You probably wouldn't get anything to eat in this building, but could you describe the '*flavour*' of the experience?

Chapter 5 The Christian Church

Learning intentions

In this chapter we will be learning:

▶ to consider how the Christian Church began

▶ to become familiar with the details of Pentecost

▶ to understand the concept of 'community' and how this was expressed in the Early Church

▶ to appreciate that the Christian Church, throughout history, required organisation in the form of leadership and creeds

▶ to investigate various styles of worship in different Churches

▶ to consider declining church attendance in Northern Ireland.

5.1 Pentecost

Think of a new experience that you have really looked forward to – something that you believed would be a great adventure. The thought of it was very exciting, but it also made you a bit nervous because you were not quite sure what to expect.

Some of you might have felt like this when you were changing school. You were looking forward to the new adventures that 'big' school would bring, but you worried all summer about exactly what it would be like. Lots of people told you it would be great and you would love it, but you didn't quite believe them.

The disciples felt like this at the time of Pentecost. Jesus had died, risen from the dead and then ascended into heaven. Now they felt alone and afraid. Jesus had promised to send them a helper. That sounded good but they didn't know what he would be like or how he would help. However, they were soon to find out.

What is Pentecost?

A Jewish festival when Jews thank God for His goodness to them, particularly thanking Him for His goodness in providing the harvest. It is also a time when Jews thank God for giving them the commandments by which to live.

5.1 Pentecost

What a transformation

The disciples went from being afraid to being powerful speakers who influenced and changed people's lives. Peter spoke to the crowd who had gathered to celebrate the Jewish Pentecost festival. Three thousand people believed what he said about Jesus and were baptised.

Many people regard Pentecost as the beginning of the Christian Church. On that day a small group of believers multiplied, and they continued to grow throughout history into the Church that we have today.

Get Active 1

Read Acts 2: 1–15.

Illustrate the events of Pentecost in a storyboard. Each picture should have a statement that describes what is happening.

Or

Write a newspaper report that describes what it might have been like to have been present at Pentecost.

Transformations today

Ivan Thompson
Ivan grew up in West Belfast. As a young adult, Ivan began betting on horses. He lost a lot of money, and eventually became addicted to gambling. In order to fund his habit, Ivan had to turn to stealing. He started to steal from those he regarded as rich – residents of the Upper Cavehill Road and the Malone Road, Belfast. After around nine months, the police eventually caught Ivan and he was sent to prison. After he was released, life continued to be difficult for Ivan. His marriage was in crisis, and he was unhappy. His only pleasures were drinking and gambling. Ivan's wife during this time became a Christian. Ivan laughed at her for doing so.

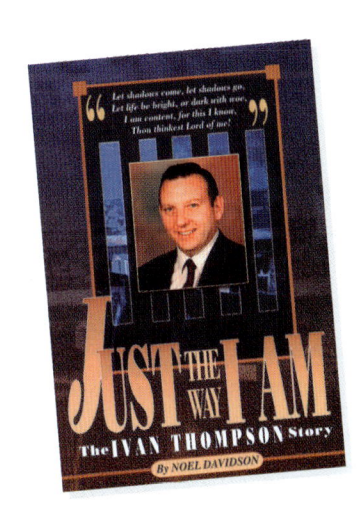

67

Chapter 5 The Christian Church

After weeks and months of persuasion, eventually Ivan agreed to go to church with his wife. There he learned that he was loved by God. He decided that he too should become a Christian. He eventually became a preacher and has encouraged many others to turn to God.

C.S. Lewis

C.S. Lewis grew up in East Belfast. At age thirteen, he declared himself an atheist (someone who doesn't believe in God). He became interested in mythology and the occult. He argued with friends that God did not exist. He viewed religion as an unnecessary chore. Lewis was a clever boy who enjoyed studying. As an adult, Lewis took up a job as a lecturer in Oxford. There he developed a friendship with J.R.R. Tolkien. Tolkien encouraged Lewis to think about faith. Slowly Lewis' thinking changed and he decided to put his faith in God. Lewis began to write Christian books (like *Surprised by Joy*). He decided to use his talents as a writer to teach others about Christianity. He has influenced and encouraged many children and adults through his books.

C.S. Lewis

Get Active 2

Both Ivan Thompson and C.S. Lewis came to have faith in God as a result of the influence of people that they were close to. Ivan's wife encouraged him to go to church. Lewis' friend persuaded him to rethink his ideas about the Christian faith.

Write about a situation where someone close to you has changed the way you think about a particular issue. If you can't think of one, write instead about an issue that you would like to change the attitudes of your friends or family towards.

5.2 The early Church

At Pentecost, the disciples experienced a transformation. Their fear and confusion was turned into hope, joy, courage and enthusiasm. Believers, excited about their faith in the risen Jesus, decided to meet together each week and offer praises to God. They also decided to look after one another during the week because they believed that this was a good way of following Jesus' example for living.

We read in the book of Acts the story of what life was like for these believers:

> *They devoted themselves to the apostles' teaching and to the fellowship, to the breaking of bread and to prayer. Everyone was filled with awe, and many wonders and miraculous signs were done by the apostles. All the believers were together and had everything in common. Selling their possessions and goods, they gave to anyone as he had need. Every day they continued to meet together in the temple courts. They broke bread in their homes and ate together with glad and sincere hearts, praising God and enjoying the favour of all the people. And the Lord added to their number daily those who were being saved.*
> ACTS 2: 42–47

Get Active 1

The group of believers who met together formed a 'community'. Communities can take different forms. One way of defining a community is 'a group of people who have shared interests or beliefs; they may live in an area close to each other'.

1. List all the things that you think were good about the Early Church community.
2. People in our society are attracted to 'good' communities. What do you think are the characteristics of a good school community? Are there things that could be changed in your school to make it a better community?

Communities continue to be important to believers today. They are places where Christians can meet with others who share their faith – for support, friendship and encouragement.

69

Chapter 5 The Christian Church

It is hard, however, to imagine that in our society there could be communities like the one described in Acts, where people share all they own, selling their belongings to help out others.

Yet, there are those who try to do so. In Holy Cross Monastery, Rostrevor, there are monks who seek to spend their whole lives in community with others who want to worship God. They choose to make a total offering of their being to God and to the community. This means they do not claim private ownership of any possessions – everything they have is shared. These men have decided to dedicate their lives to prayer, serving others and helping to promote peace and unity in Northern Ireland.

Holy Cross Monastery

Get Active 2

Look at the daily routine of the monks at Holy Cross.

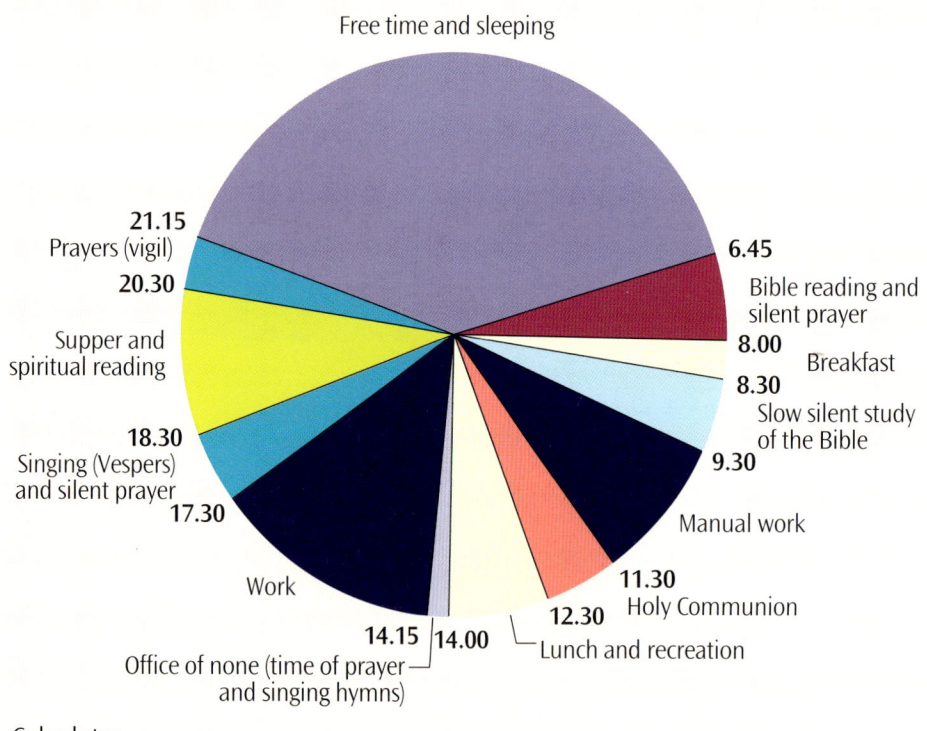

Pie chart showing daily schedule:
- Free time and sleeping
- 6.45 Bible reading and silent prayer
- 8.00 Breakfast
- 8.30 Slow silent study of the Bible
- 9.30 Manual work
- 11.30 Holy Communion
- 12.30 Lunch and recreation
- 14.00 / 14.15 Office of none (time of prayer and singing hymns)
- 17.30 Work
- 18.30 Singing (Vespers) and silent prayer
- 20.30 Supper and spiritual reading
- 21.15 Prayers (vigil)

What part of the day do you think you would find most difficult?

Calculate:

▶ How long do the monks spend each day at work?

▶ How long do they spend studying the Bible or other spiritual books?

▶ How long do they spend in prayer?

5.3 Getting organised

Communities need to be organised so that the people who belong to them can work together successfully. You can imagine the difficulties, for example, in a community where there are no clear rules and no clear leaders.

For the first 300 years of the Church's existence it faced persecution, and many Christians were killed because of their beliefs. Christians met in the open air or in houses to worship as they could not afford to build churches. They also believed that Jesus would return to Earth, leading to the end of the world, and therefore they did not think it was necessary to build places of worship. However, they soon realised organisation was needed.

One way of keeping the Church organised was to appoint leaders. These leaders would help look after community life and could help deal with disputes should they arise.

Another way of keeping the Church organised at a time when few people could read or write was to develop and teach statements of what the community believed. These were known as **creeds**.

The Council of Nicaea

One of the emperors of the Roman Empire in the fourth century was Constantine. Constantine believed it was important that the Christian Church was united. He decided to call together the first ecumenical (worldwide) council of the Christian Church in a place called Nicaea. Those who met there discussed the key beliefs of the Church, and at the end of their discussion they created the first Christian creed. It is called the Nicene Creed, which was later developed and is still used today, particularly in the Eastern Christian Churches.

Chapter 5 The Christian Church

The Apostles' Creed

The most commonly used creed in Western Churches is the Apostles' Creed. A form of this creed was in use almost 200 years before the Nicene Creed. It was used as a declaration of faith before a person was baptised. It was given the name of 'Apostles' Creed' as legend states that it was first put together by the twelve apostles. The version used in Churches today was written in the eighth century.

Get Active 1

Read the Apostles' Creed opposite:

1. Read the Apostles' Creed carefully and discuss with your teacher any parts you don't understand.

2. Work with a partner. Think of five questions that could be answered by reading the Apostles' Creed. For example: What do you believe about God? Answer: There is one God, who made the Earth and heaven and everything seen and unseen.

3. Swap your five questions with another group. Now try answering their questions using the Apostles' Creed to help you.

4. Share your questions and answers with the class. Discuss with the class whether they agree with the answers to the questions that have been given.

THE APOSTLES' CREED

I believe in God, the Father almighty, creator of heaven and earth.

I believe in Jesus Christ, his only Son, our Lord, who was conceived by the Holy Spirit, born of the Virgin Mary, suffered under Pontius Pilate, was crucified, died, and was buried; he descended into hell.
On the third day he rose again; he ascended into heaven, he is seated at the right hand of the Father, and he will come to judge the living and the dead.

I believe in the Holy Spirit, the holy catholic Church, the communion of saints, the forgiveness of sins, the resurrection of the body, and the life everlasting.

Amen.

Key words

Descended – went downwards
Ascended – went upwards
Conceived – became pregnant
Resurrection – being raised from the dead
Catholic – the word 'catholic' refers not to the Roman Catholic Church, but to the universal church of Jesus

5.4 Full of diversity

You are part of your school community. But your school community is not the only community you belong to. What others are you part of?

Think of the different ways that you behave in the different communities you are part of. There are different dress codes in each – you may have a uniform for school, a kit for hockey, a costume for swimming club. There are different rules – you have to sit quietly in church, you are supposed to shout to encourage your team mates on the rugby pitch. You may communicate with members of different communities in different ways. Think of how you speak differently to your teachers, parents, friends.

The Christian Church is one large community, with many shared beliefs. However, within that community there is also much diversity. There are small churches and large churches. There are formal Christian communities and ones that are much more informal. There are churches that have lots of young people and churches with very few young people at all.

Let us look briefly at some of the different churches in our country:

> ### Key word
> **Denomination** – a group of congregations, united by a common faith and name, which has its own distinctive form of organisation.

▶ 1 **Belfast Cathedral**

   Denomination: Church of Ireland

   Services on Sunday: 10.00 am, 11.00 am and 3.30 pm

   Other activities: Healing services, prayer meetings

   Music: Choral music, organ

   Web address: www.belfastcathedral.org

Belfast Cathedral

Chapter 5 The Christian Church

▶ **2 Strandtown Christian Fellowship Church**

Denomination: Non-denominational

Services on Sunday: 9.30 am, 11.30 am and 7.00 pm

Other activities: Crèche, kids' club, mothers and toddlers, youth events, cell groups, teaching and training, counselling, prayer groups, healing ministry

Music: Modern music, led by a variety of bands

Web address: www.cfc-net.org

Strandtown Christian Fellowship Church

▶ **3 St Anthony's Catholic Church**

Denomination: Roman Catholic

Services on Sunday: 7.00 am, 9.30 am, 11.00 am and 12.30 pm

Other activities: School retreats, youth missions, 'StreetReach', discussion groups, midweek services, confession, special talks, counselling

Music: Choral music, organ

Web address: www.saintanthony.co.uk

St Anthony's Catholic Church

Get Active 1

Produce a leaflet using ICT to advertise one of the churches on the last two pages. Include information about the church building, the minister, the times of the services, the other activities offered by the church, the church's address and contact numbers. Try to present this leaflet as creatively as possible. Remember that the purpose of the leaflet is to attract people to attend the church.

5.5 A dying community?

Fifty years ago, the church was the centre of community life in Northern Ireland. Almost everyone went to church, was involved in church activities and knew the other members of their congregation. Ministers were treated with respect and were consulted widely on issues that concerned the community.

Today this has all changed. Only three in ten people attend church regularly. All the major denominations in Northern Ireland report declining numbers. The average age of membership in Churches is increasing.

Get Active 1

Answer the following questions:

- Why do you think that many people do not attend church on a Sunday?
- Do you think that Church is an outdated organisation? Explain your answer.

Many young people regard church as irrelevant to their lives. They find it difficult to relate to Sunday services. They find sermons hard to understand. Many think that there are much better ways to spend their Sundays than by attending church.

Chapter 5 The Christian Church

Here are the words of some young people who were asked to give their opinion on 'church':

Quote 1

> I think church is important, but I do find it boring because it is directed towards adults. I enjoy the youth church, however.

Quote 2

> I have been to church only a couple of times, sometimes for a Sunday service and once for a funeral. I find church boring, single-minded and dusty. I don't find it interactive or engrossing.

Quote 3

> I don't believe in organised religion. I prefer to praise and worship God in my own way at home.

Get Active 2

Conduct a class survey. First, gather information on the following issues:

- ▶ How many people attend church every Sunday?
- ▶ How many people only attend occasionally?
- ▶ How many people never go to church?
- ▶ How many people attend church events?
- ▶ Which events do they attend?

Then illustrate your results in two pie charts – one for church attendance on Sundays, one for attendance of church organisations.

5.5 A dying community

There's still hope

The late Archbishop Oscar Romero once said, 'The Church, with its message, with its word, will meet a thousand obstacles, just as the river encounters boulders, rocks, chasms. No matter; the river carries a promise: "I will be with you to the end of the ages" and the gates of hell shall not prevail against the will of God.'

Romero believed that the Church would never die, and that church members should do all in their power to reach out to others with the message of Jesus. Many Christians agree with Romero's attitude and are seeking to encourage family, friends and colleagues to think about attending church. Many churches are also trying to provide a variety of organisations for children, teenagers and adults to attract them to the church community.

Mural of Oscar Romero

Summary

- ▶ The Christian Church was born at Pentecost.
- ▶ The Early Church is an example of a community that worked together for the good of all its members.
- ▶ Throughout the history of the Church, it has been important for Christians to set out what they believe. One way they have done this is through writing creeds.
- ▶ The Christian Church is full of diversity and contains many different denominations.
- ▶ Church attendance in Northern Ireland is declining.

Chapter 5 The Christian Church

The Christian Church: The big task

Having completed the chapter on 'The Christian Church', complete the following tasks:

Task 1

Match the words with their definitions:

1 Vow of poverty	a) An example of one is the Presbyterian Church. This word describes a group of churches who have shared beliefs and are organised by a form of church government.
2 Creed	b) A Jewish festival which celebrated God's goodness in providing for people through the harvest.
3 Pentecost	c) A group of people who live in the same area or who have similar interests or beliefs. An example could be a football club.
4 Denomination	d) One of the promises made by monks or nuns before they enter a monastery or convent. This is a promise to share all that they own with the other members of the community.
5 Community	e) A statement that outlines a set of beliefs that a person or group of people may have.

Task 2

1. Consider in groups whether there are ways in which Church leaders could change church services and church communities to make them more appealing to young people. What ideas can you come up with?

2. Use your ideas to create an advertising poster that you think would market a church effectively to young people. Here's an example that one church congregation tried.

Chapter 6
Judaism

▶ With a partner write down what you know about this symbol.
▶ Think about things such as its name, where you might find it, what it has been used for, why it is a symbol of the Jewish faith.
▶ Write down any other symbols you know that are used within the Jewish faith. Why might these symbols be used?
▶ Share your thoughts with the rest of the class.

Chapter 6 Judaism

Learning intentions

By the end of this chapter:

▶ you will have explored the history of the Jewish community in Northern Ireland

▶ you will have discovered some of the key beliefs within Judaism

▶ you will have researched the Jewish place of worship

▶ you will have examined the Jewish festival Passover

▶ you will have explored the Bar Mitzvah, a Jewish rite of passage.

6.1 Introduction

Famous Jewish people

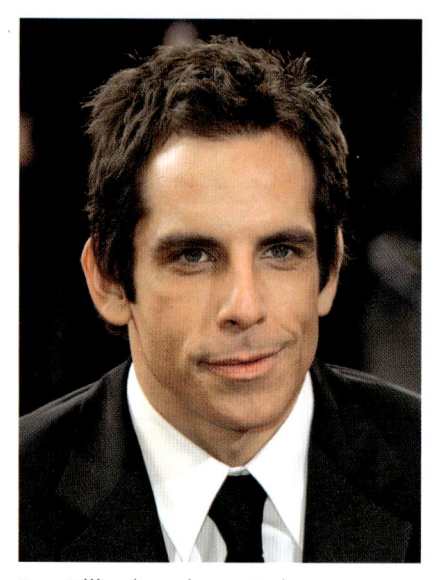

Ben Stiller *(American actor)*

David Schwimmer *(American actor)*

Sacha Baron Cohen *(British comedian and actor)*

6.1 Introduction

Get Active 1

Think, pair, share

1. In your workbook, write down everything that you associate with the word 'Jew'.

2. Share these things with your partner and explain why you have written them.

3. Report back to the class two things that your partner chose and explain why.

4. Now copy and complete the What I Know, What I Want to Know and What I Have Learned grid below. Under the heading What I Know, write down everything that you already know about the Jewish faith. Under the heading What I Want to Know, write down what you would like to learn about the Jewish faith. At the end of this chapter, write down what you have learned.

What I Know	What I Want to Know	What I Have Learned

Jews in Northern Ireland

▶ Belfast has a small Jewish population of approximately four hundred people and it is led by a rabbi. **Rabbi** is the name given to the leader of a Jewish synagogue. The word 'rabbi' means teacher.

▶ There are no other Jewish communities in Northern Ireland.

▶ At one time there were well over 2000 Jews in Northern Ireland and from this community Sir Otto Jaffe was twice elected Lord Mayor of Belfast. He presented the city with the Jaffe fountain as a symbol of the enormous contribution Jews made to the commercial, political, arts and educational life of Belfast. It was returned to its original place at Victoria Shopping centre in 2008.

▶ The 'troubles' led to many Jews leaving Belfast and going to live in the south of Ireland, England, Israel and America.

▶ The Belfast Hebrew congregation was first founded in 1869.

▶ The Jewish Synagogue was built in 1964 and can be found on the Somerton Road, Belfast.

Chapter 6 Judaism

6.2 Key beliefs

Sit quietly. For a few minutes, consider some of the things that are most important to you. Who are the people or things that you value most? What issues do you feel strongly about? What activities do you value most? Share some of the things that you have been considering with the rest of your class.

There are a number of important ideas that all Jews regard as significant. They are summarised below:

Key beliefs in Judaism

Scripture
Jews believe that the **Torah** is very important. The Torah is the name given to the five books: Genesis, Exodus, Leviticus, Numbers and Deuteronomy. Jews believe that these are books which God gave to His people to teach them how to live. The **Ten Commandments** are considered the most important commandments of the Torah.

God
Jews believe that there is **one God**, who created the universe, and yet has a concern for individuals and their lives.

After death
In Judaism, death is viewed, not as a tragedy, but as an important part of being human. Jews believe that people who have lived good lives will be rewarded by God in heaven.

Being chosen
Jews believe that they are God's chosen people. They believe that God made a promise to a man called Abraham – that his people would be a great nation. Jews believe that they are these people, descendants of Abraham.

Messiah
Jews believe God is going to send a special person who will establish God's Kingdom on earth. They call him the **Messiah**. The word Messiah means 'a saviour; a deliverer; one who protects you from danger'.

Family life
The family and community are very important within Jewish life. Worship in the home is a special part of Jewish life. At the doorpost of a Jewish home there is a **Mezuzah**. A Mezuzah is a small case that contains a prayer and a commandment. The prayer states 'Hear, O Israel, The Lord our God is one. Love the Lord your God with all your heart and all your mind and all your strength. Never forget these commands, teach them to your children. Repeat them when you are at home and when you are away. Tie them on your arm and on your forehead as a reminder. Write them on the doorposts of your house.' (Deuteronomy 6: 4–9)

6.2 Key beliefs

Get Active 1

1. Look at the key beliefs outlined in the spider diagram opposite. Spend time reading them over and trying to commit as many of the key ideas as possible to memory. After two minutes your teacher will ask you to close your book. He/she will then pick two people from your class to come to the front. Your task is to ask those pupils three factual questions about the information that you have learned. How many do they get right?

2. Jesus, the man whom Christians regard as the Messiah promised from God, was a Jew. Christianity grew out of a Jewish background. Given this background, there are a number of common beliefs that Jews and Christians share. There are also, however, differences. Copy and complete the table below, using the information that you know about Jews and Christians.

Key issues	Jewish beliefs	Christian beliefs
God		
Scripture		
Messiah		

Get Active 2

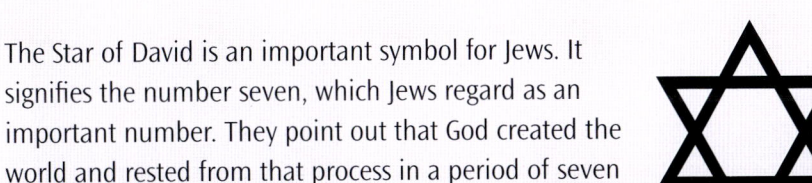

The Star of David is an important symbol for Jews. It signifies the number seven, which Jews regard as an important number. They point out that God created the world and rested from that process in a period of seven days. They believe that there are seven spirits of God.

The Star reminds Jews of their identity as God's people and the importance of trusting in Him.

Draw a Star of David in your exercise book. In the centre write 'Important Jewish beliefs'. In the points of the star write, in your own words, six key beliefs in Judaism.

Chapter 6 Judaism

6.3 The synagogue

Synagogue means 'house of assembly'. It is the name given to the Jewish place of worship. Every **Shabbat**, most Jewish people will go to the synagogue to worship God together. Shabbat is the Jewish holy day which begins at sunset on Friday until sunset on Saturday.

Belfast Synagogue

Get Active 1

Research

Find out more about Shabbat. Go to the website www.akhlah.com and click on Shabbat. Read the information and write down five to ten things that happen on Shabbat. Share this information with a partner. Together design an information poster which explains what happens on Shabbat.

Most synagogues are built facing towards Jerusalem and have a similar layout inside. At the entrance there are sinks for the worshippers to wash their hands. They do this to show that they are ready for prayer. The men and women then go and sit in separate areas. At the front of the synagogue there is a large cupboard covered by a screen. The cupboard is called the **Ark** and kept inside are the scrolls of the Torah, the holiest object in the synagogue.

A lamp is in front of the Ark and it is never allowed to go out. This reminds the people of the longevity and infinity of God.

The Ark

The lamp

6.3 The synagoue

In the centre of the synagogue is a raised platform called a **Bimah**. The scrolls are brought from the Ark, placed on the table and read from here.

Jews believe that worshipping God is very important and that they can worship God anywhere. Throughout the week they are expected to pray three times a day and some Jews will go to the synagogue to do this. However, on Shabbat most Jews will attend the synagogue to worship together. The service is usually led by a rabbi and includes readings from the scriptures, prayers, singing of hymns and a sermon. Some of the Torah, the first five books of the Old Testament, may also be read.

The Bimah

The scrolls

Get Active 2

Go to the following website, www.hitchams.suffolk.sch.uk/synagogue, where a virtual synagogue will appear. Explore this synagogue and listen to the different people explaining what various items are.

Prayer is a significant part of Jewish worship. One of the most important Jewish prayers is the **Shema**. This will be said three times a day during regular prayers and it is usually said during synagogue worship.

The Shema reminds Jews that:

▶ There is only one God.
▶ God is good and loves them and they should love Him.
▶ God's rules apply to every part of a person's life.
▶ Children should be taught about the Torah.

Chapter 6 Judaism

The Shema

Hear, O Israel, The LORD our God, the LORD is One. Love the LORD your God with all your heart and with all your soul and with all your strength. These commandments that I give you today are to be upon your hearts. Impress them on your children. Talk about them when you sit at home and when you walk along the road, when you lie down and when you get up. Tie them as symbols on your hands and bind them on your foreheads. Write them on the door-frames of your houses and on your gates.

DEUTERONOMY 6: 4–9

Men wear special clothes for prayers. They wear a **kippah** (skull cap) on their head to show respect for God and a **tallit** (a prayer robe) around their shoulders. The fringes on the end of the tallit are knotted to remind Jews of the laws of the Torah. The **Tefillin** is a small box which is strapped to their forehead and left arm. Inside the box are writings from the Torah. They are strapped to their forehead to remind them to keep God's law in their head; and on their left arm, facing the heart, to remind them to keep God's law in their heart.

A young Jewish boy reading the Torah. Can you see the Tefillin on his forehead and left arm?

6.4 Important festivals (Passover)

- What sort of pictures and images are conjured up in your mind when you hear the word 'festival'?
- Festivals are usually considered to be times of joy, celebration, time with family, good food, presents! Jewish festivals include all of these elements.
- There are a number of important festivals in the Jewish year. One of the most important is the celebration and commemoration of the Passover.

The history of the Passover

Passover (Pesach in Hebrew) is the time when Jewish people remember how the people of God left slavery behind them when they fled from Egypt. The story of their release is a remarkable one. Here are some of the highlights of the story below.

- The Israelites came to live in a land called Egypt. Initially, they were treated well. So they multiplied in number and settled there.
- However, the leader of the region, Pharaoh, was worried that if the Israelites grew much larger in number, they might try to take over the land. To ensure this would not happen, Pharaoh decided to begin treating the Jews as slaves.
- Moses was an Israelite to whom God appeared in the form of a burning bush. God told Moses to tell Pharaoh to let His people leave the country. Moses did what God asked. He took his brother Aaron with him to help him.
- Pharaoh refused to do as Moses asked.
- God sent ten different plagues to punish the Egyptians for not giving the Israelites their freedom. After each plague, Moses pleaded with Pharaoh to release his people. Each time Pharaoh refused. The plagues included frogs, hail, locusts, darkness and rivers of blood.

Chapter 6 Judaism

- The final plague was the most horrific. This plague was the death of all firstborn boys in Egypt. Israelite families were spared this horror if they killed a lamb and spread its blood on the doorpost of their house.

- When Pharaoh's son died, he knew that God must be very powerful and he feared what else God might do. He let the Israelites leave Egypt. This event is known as the **Exodus**.

Get Active 1

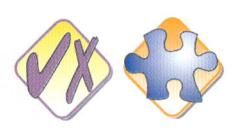

1 Think about how different life would be if you didn't have your own freedom. Discuss with a partner some of the ways your life would change if you were forced to become a slave.

2 When we try to put ourselves in the shoes of another person, this is called **empathy**. Your task here is to complete a piece of empathetic writing. Try to put yourself in the shoes of the Jewish slaves. Imagine that your family are all slaves in Egypt. Imagine that, even though you are young, you are forced to work long hours, doing hard manual work every day. Imagine that you have heard that your family will be released from slavery if you spread blood on the doorpost of your house. Write a diary entry in which you record some of your feelings and thoughts about your captors and your hopes about a new life of freedom.

The celebration of Passover

The Passover is celebrated by Jews in March/April. The festival lasts for seven days. During this time, Jews have to ensure that there is nothing in the house that contains **yeast**. Yeast is an ingredient that is used in the baking of bread to make the bread rise. Jews believe that removing this ingredient from their houses helps to remind them that the Jews leaving Egypt were in a hurry, and did not have time to let their bread rise. It is also a symbolic way of challenging them to ensure that they remove the 'chometz' (the wrong things) from their lives.

6.4 Important festivals (Passover)

The highlight of the Passover celebrations is the **Seder meal**. This is shared by families and friends on the first night of Passover. During this meal, Jews believe that the food that they eat, and the way that they eat the food, represent key aspects of the story of the first Passover.

Look at the diagram below. It shows the important things that are eaten at the Seder meal. It also gives you information on why each of these items is important.

Haroseth – There are different Haroseth recipes, but usually Haroseth is a mixture of nuts, cinnamon and apples that represent the materials used by the Jews to make bricks for the Egyptians.

Parsley – This is dipped in salt water during the meal. The parsley reminds Jews of their poverty as slaves in Egypt and the salt water reminds them of the tears they cried during this time.

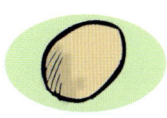

An egg – This is a symbol of new life – the new life of freedom that the Jews gained once they were freed from slavery.

A Seder meal

Shank bone – This represents the lamb that was sacrificed on the night that the Angel of Death passed over Egypt.

Bitter herbs – These represent the horrendous conditions of slavery and the bitterness that the Jews felt towards their masters, the Egyptians.

Get Active 2

1 Spend three minutes looking at the diagram of the Seder meal. Read the labels and try to memorise them. Once your three minutes are up, close your textbook and try to draw the diagram from memory.

2 How close is your drawing to the original diagram?

You could try this task again at the start of your next lesson. This time you will only get one and a half minutes to remind yourself of the original diagram.

6.5 Bar Mitzvah

Within the Jewish faith there is a special service that marks the beginning of adulthood. From this time onwards a young person is expected to fulfil the law of the Torah on their own. It is called a **Bar Mitzvah**, which means 'son of the commandment', and has existed for as long as the Torah.

When a Jewish boy turns thirteen he is considered to have reached adulthood. This means that he is now responsible for his own actions. Jewish families celebrate the boy's thirteenth birthday with a party. On the following Shabbat his Bar Mitzvah will take place in the synagogue. He will no longer sit with the women and children but will be allowed to sit with the men. He will wear for the first time the special prayer clothes and he will be asked to read from the Torah. The Torah is always read in Hebrew and the boy will have spent a lot of time preparing for this event. Once he has read the Torah his father will thank God for his son and the Rabbi may say some words of encouragement to him during his sermon.

Family and friends are invited to the Bar Mitzvah and a small party is held afterwards. The boy gives a speech thanking his parents for all that they have done, and he accepts the responsibilities of an adult Jew. Presents will also be given at this time.

Bat Mitzvah

In recent years many Jewish families have begun to mark a girl becoming an adult with a **Bat Mitzvah** – 'daughter of the commandment'. A girl is considered to have entered adulthood by the age of twelve, and on the Shabbat after her twelfth birthday she will have her Bat Mitzvah.

Is becoming an adult celebrated in your family? What age do you become an adult? How is it celebrated? Can you think of any ceremonies that take place in a Christian Church that mark moving from childhood to adulthood?

6.5 Bar Mitzah

This boy and his family are celebrating his Bar Mitzvah

Get Active 1

1 In the past when a boy turned thirteen he was recognised as an adult but there was no Bar Mitzvah. Why do you think it was decided to have a special ceremony to mark this occasion?

2 Imagine you were having your Bar Mitzvah or Bat Mitzvah.

▶ How would you have prepared for it? Think about what you would need to know and what you would be wearing.

▶ How would you be feeling on that morning and why?

▶ What would you be looking forward to the most on that day and why?

Chapter 6 Judaism

Judaism: The big task

Having completed the chapter on 'Judaism', complete the following task:

Below are the answers to some questions about Judaism. Your task is to create the questions that could go with each answer. Try to make your questions imaginative and different from those of others in the class.

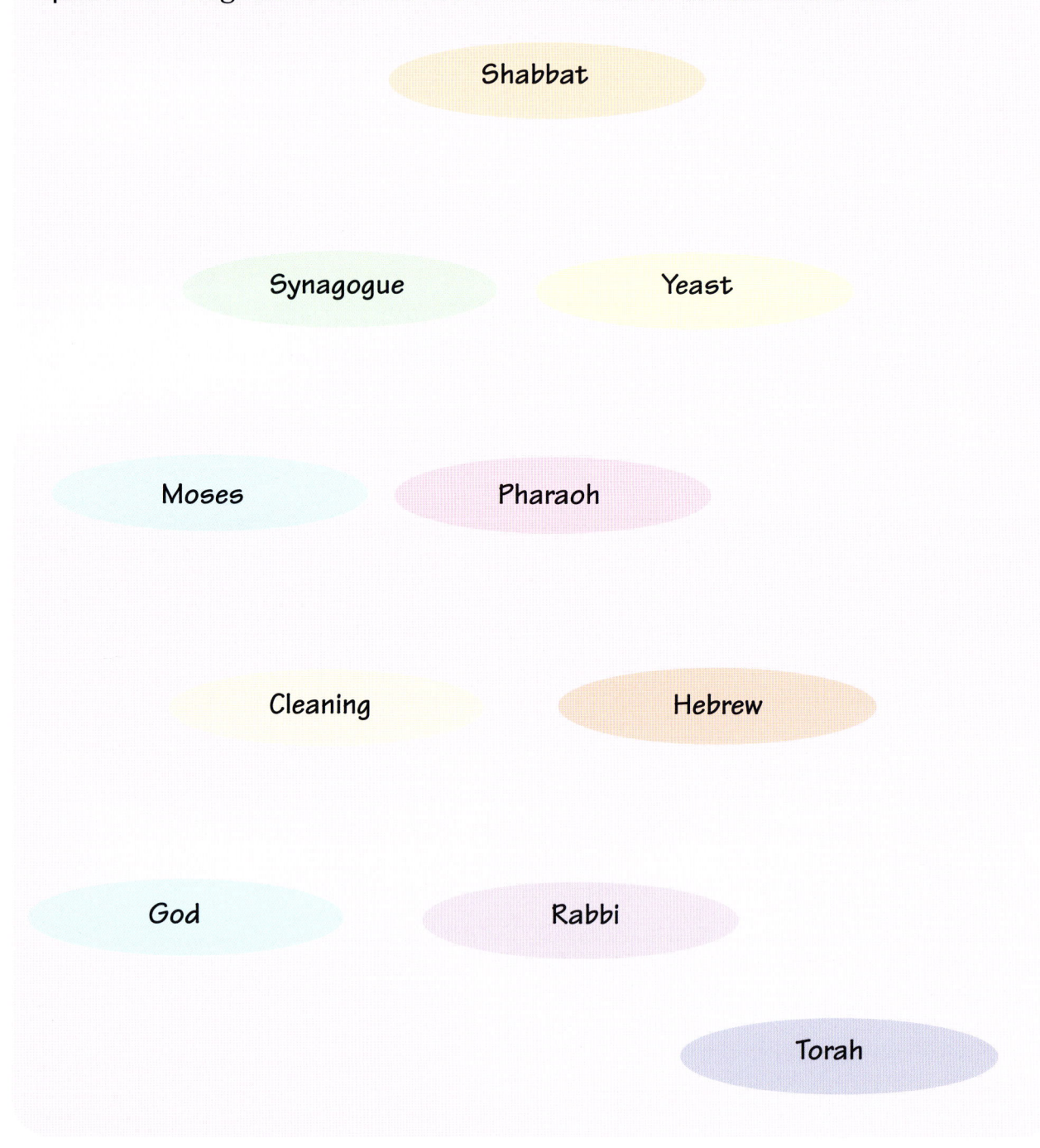

- Shabbat
- Synagogue
- Yeast
- Moses
- Pharaoh
- Cleaning
- Hebrew
- God
- Rabbi
- Torah

Glossary

A

arrogance – to be proud and overbearing

B

Bar Mitzvah – a special service that marks the beginning of adulthood

Bat Mitzvah – the Bar Mitzvah for a girl

C

community – group of people

creed – a formal statement of religious belief

D

denomination – sect of religious believers

E

epistles – letters

Exodus – when the Israelites left Egypt

F

faith – strong belief in someone or something

faithful – loyal

famine – occurs when there is a drastic shortage of food

G

gleaning – to gather up left-over crops that harvesters leave behind

gospels – the first four books of the New Testament, meaning 'good news'

H

Hesed – loving kindness

I

identity – the characteristics by which an individual is recognisable

interpret – to explain the meaning of something

Israelites – the name given to the people of the Jewish nation

K

kippah – Jewish skull cap

M

Messiah – means a saviour; a deliverer; one who protects you from danger

Mezuzah – a small case that contains some scriptures

O

obedience – to carry out instructions willingly

P

Passover – Jewish festival celebrating the exodus of the Israelites from Egypt

Pentateuch – the first five books of the Old Testament

Pentecost – Jewish festival of thanksgiving

prophecy – to predict something

R

rabbi – the leader of a Jewish synagogue

resurrection – rising again

S

Seder meal – a meal shared by families and friends on the first night of Passover

self-image – perception of oneself

Shabbat – the Jewish holy day

Shema – one of the most important Jewish prayers

synagogue – the Jewish place of worship

T

tallit – Jewish prayer robe

Tefillin – a small box which Jews strap to their forehead and left arm; inside the box are writings from the Torah

Torah – the five books: Genesis, Exodus, Leviticus, Numbers and Deuteronomy

trust – to believe in and rely on

Index

A
artists 29

B
Bar Mitzvah 90–91
Bat Mitzvah 90
beautiful in the eyes of God 14
Belfast Cathedral 73
Bible
    Acts of the Apostles 28, 69
    books of the 27–29
    Corinthians 11
    Deuteronomy 27, 86
    importance to Christians 22–23
    interesting facts 27
    Isaiah 53
    James 11
    and the love of God 8, 30–32, 45
    Luke 61
    making sacrifices to spread the 21
    Mark 59, 63
    Micah 53
    on pride and boasting 11
    Proverbs 11
    Psalms 16, 23, 28, 31
    Revelation 29
    Samuel 13, 27
    Ten Commandments 43, 66, 82
    and who we are 8, 16, 17
Blondin 41

C
Casting Crowns 8
Christian Church
    attitudes of young people 75–76
    beginning of the 66–68
    declining attendance 75–77
    diversity of the 73–74
    early 69–70
    inside a 65
    organisation 71–72
Christmas 53, 63
communities 69–70, 71, 73
comparing oneself to others 15–17
Constantine, Emperor 71
Coren, Michael 14
Council of Nicaea 71
Creation of Adam, The 29
creeds 71–72

D
denomination 73
disciples 56–58, 66–67, 72
Duduman, Dumitru 21

E
Egypt, flight from 87–88

F
faith 41
faithfulness 38–40
famine 38

G
Gideons International 24–26

H
Harry Potter and the Deathly Hallows 15
Hesed 47
Holy Cross Monastery 70

I
identity 7
interpretation 23
Israelites 27, 28, 87–88

J
Jaffe, Sir Otto 81
Jesus
    birth 52–53
    death 31, 62–63
    mission 54–55
    picking His twelve disciples 56–58
    power 59–61
    thinking of 50–51
Jesus Walks 49
John 29, 56
Judaism 79–92
    Bar Mitzvah 90–91
    importance of Hesed 47
    intolerance of outsiders 44
    Jews in Northern Ireland 81
    key beliefs 82–83
    men's clothing for prayers 86
    Passover 87–89
    Star of David 83
    the synagogue 84–86
Judas 57

L
Lewis, C.S. 62, 63, 68
Lion, the Witch and the Wardrobe, The 62–63
love
    of God 8, 30–32, 45
    for those who are different 44–47
loving kindness 47

Index

M
Messiah 82
Mezuzah 82
Michelangelo 29
miracles 59–61
Moses 27, 87
Mother Teresa 14

O
obedience 42
outsiders, loving 44–47

P
Passover 87–89
Paul 28, 29
Pentateuch 27
Pentecost 65–68
persecution 21, 71

Peter 28, 29, 56, 58, 67
Pharaoh 87, 88
poor people 54, 59
prophecies 29, 53
prophets 28

R
Rabbi 81, 90
Religious Education 2–4
Revelation 29
role models 55
Romero, Archbishop Oscar 77
Rowling, J.K. 15
Ruth, the story of 36–39, 42–47

S
sacrifices, making 21, 31, 62, 63
Seder meal 89

self-image 10–14
Shema 85–86
St Anthony's Catholic Church 74
Strandtown Christian Fellowship Church 74
synagogues 81, 84–86

T
Thompson, Ivan 67–68
Torah 82, 84, 86, 90
transformations 67–68, 69
trust 41–43

W
West, Kanye 49
Who am I 9